The Way To Happiness: My Journey

ADELE RODRIGUEZ

Copyright © 2015 by Adele Rodriguez

The Way To Happiness: My Journey
by Adele Rodriguez

Printed in the United States of America.

ISBN 9781498451901

All rights reserved solely by the author. The author guarantees all contents are original and do not infringe upon the legal rights of any other person or work. No part of this book may be reproduced in any form without the permission of the author. The views expressed in this book are not necessarily those of the publisher.

Scripture quotations taken from the Amplified Bible (AMP). Copyright © 1954, 1958, 1962, 1964, 1965, 1987 by The Lockman Foundation. Used by permission. All rights reserved.

www.xulonpress.com

I dedicate this book to my Lord and Savior for his many answered prayers and to my husband Jay for his unwavering love and support through the years which inspired and motivated me to write this book in the hope that others might find my way to happiness.

Table Of Contents

Introduction: Try My Way ix

CHAPTERS
1. Don't Feel Guilty About Loving Yourself 19
2. Find Happiness In Giving Happiness 29
3. Do Unto Others… 36
4. Just Look Around You 45
5. Organize And Act Out Your Dreams 49
6. Give It All You Got 66
7. Who's Perfect? Keep At It! 71
8. Keep Busy 78
9. Two Magic Words: "I'm Sorry" 86
10. Callous Your Feelings 90
11. Keep Your Cool 98
12. Here And Now 106
13. Some Rain Must Fall In Every Life,
    Prayer Is The Answer 113
14. Woman And Man 151
15. Marriage: Our Most Exciting Challenge 164
16. People Molding: Our Most Creative Challenge 182
17. Words To Future Parents 191

18. The Quest For Happiness Of The
    Working Woman And Mate 194
19. As You Up In Years, Stay Young At Heart 210
20. Don't Tell Me You Can't Change.................... 217

INTRODUCTION

Try My Way

People often wonder: what is happiness? Probably no other human feeling is so difficult to define as it can mean many things to different people when considered at a superficial level. But, much deeper, a common denominator seems to be a permanent feeling of contentment, peace, and serenity, mixed with enthusiasm to live and faith in the future. This deep feeling of true happiness which lingers with you even when times may be rough and tough should not be confused with the transitory state of joy and exhilaration that everyone experiences at times but leaves a feeling of emptiness once it has passed. Anything that can genuinely produce this deep and lasting feeling in us is worth pursuing.

There may be many roads to happiness, and I am not implying that what has given me happiness will make everyone happy, if their values are different from mine. But, if what you are doing now is not creating in you this wonderful feeling that stays with you, not for a day, or a week, but always, then perhaps it's time to make some changes in your life and your values and to experiment with various basic principles that can produce this lasting state of contentment, peace, serenity, enthusiasm to live and faith in the future that I define as happiness. At first glance, my way may appear simple and unsophisticated, but it can lead you to the happiness that has been mine for many years. Perhaps, you may be searching through more elaborate and complex avenues for that happiness we all seek and yearn but have not yet found. Then, I encourage you to try my way to happiness.

If you have already found happiness through a way of your own which has produced the same results for you, I probably have little to offer. However, I hope I might reach many others who are still groping through life, searching incessantly, unfulfilled, unhappy, dissatisfied with themselves and others, and with life itself. I would venture to believe that most people who are feeling unhappy and miserable could also find happiness my way, if they just dared to change their values, their aspirations, and their perception of fulfillment in their lives.

After almost a lifetime with my pattern of living, I know that it works and that happiness is attainable for most of us if we are willing to change. We need to mellow, to put God in our lives and to give Him a little help by using our intelligence in eliminating obstacles from our everyday living.

I had a normal childhood. My parents were caring and gave me much love, and although I was an only child, loneliness was never a problem because I had a large and closely knitted family on my mother's side with many cousins. I grew up with one in the same household in a true brother/sister relationship, fighting one minute and buddies the next. School was fun and came easy to me. I had plenty of friends and never felt left out. Despite the extreme care of a super-protective mother who was afraid of about just everything, I somehow managed to get my share of bicycle riding, skating, swimming and play because I had a stronger will than she. However, in spite of this entire normalcy, I can recall not being completely happy and feeling deep down sad many times during those awful and frustrating growing-up years. And then, somewhere after my 15th birthday, I experienced a marked spiritual change that drew me close to God. This spiritual change was totally self-motivated as with atheistic parents I had not been brought up within a religious framework at all.

Looking back, I cannot remember exactly when this spiritual turning point in my life happened, and I started the journey which has led me to the happiness that stays with me in a beautiful, peaceful and joyful way. I believe it was in my early teens when out of fear because of a health issue, I felt a great need to connect with a higher power. God was entirely foreign to me at the time. I visualized myself alone in this huge universe battling with forces over which neither I nor my parents had control. Who could I turn to if my mother and father on whom I solely relied could not help? I believe that this sense of impotency made me turn to a God I did not know but had heard bits and pieces at school. I found my answers by talking to Him in a simple way as an adolescent would, and through Him strength and peace began to enter my spirit.

Through the years that followed, as my faith grew, I changed gradually, becoming more tolerant and understanding of others, more loving and kind, less sensitive, more enthusiastic, mellower. As I changed, doors began to open for me like magic, and life became so much easier to live. I was hardly ever faced with a challenging situation, and when one confronted me, I could handle the problem so much better. As I evolved into a new person, the new me became a very happy me.

It was not that I found instant happiness in one day, or in one month, or even one year, but with each passing day, as I filled my everyday living with more love and compassion, and these human qualities played an increasingly important part in my life, I felt happier with myself and others. I know well I am not perfect by any means, as no one is, but living close to God has helped me become a better person, and I will continue to work at this self-improvement to my very last day.

I am convinced that my close communion with God gave me the strength and power to change and guided me through my years of growth and evolution, allowing me to find happiness. I am not attempting to convert anyone into a given religion. I am simply saying that I believe we should all find God in a very personal way. I am not thinking of organized religion. I am not a member of any, but I did find God in my own personal way and through Him, I began to evaluate life differently. I found the clarity to understand much that I had been unable to comprehend before, and He helped me to reach the serenity to enjoy life with faith in the future. He has helped me at each crossroad and shown me the way clearly when I have felt confused. The events that followed each crossroad in my life are tangible proof that He guided me in the right direction.

My happy life is living proof of so many answered prayers and blessings which I have outlined throughout this book. I consider that I have a fairy tale life with 66 years of a beautiful marriage with a wonderful husband, two great daughters, and God has even blessed me with the best sons-in-law anyone can hope for. He has continued to bless me giving me four loving grandchildren that I adore and now three gorgeous great grandchildren that have added new zest to my senior years.

My work was always fulfilling, and I was always recognized and commended for my performance in my various positions which were always challenging and interesting.

I get along with people, and people are nice to me. I feel on top of the world as I begin each day with energy and a feeling of contentment with my life.

My husband and I retired at the same time, and we have enjoyed 16 years of constant togetherness, traveling, and doing the things we like. We are always active. As my husband says there is "never a dull moment" with us. Our minds are sharp, and we can handle, to some degree for our age, the new cybernetic world, paying our bills online, information searching, and emailing. I have even progressed to texting and downloading and uploading photos which I consider quite a feat at my age. It is all just beautiful!

We have never felt left out by our family. They include us in their lives and doings. Now in our 80s God has allowed us to remain independent but never cast aside as oftentimes occurs with older people.

In other words, I am a happy person.

What more happiness can anyone desire? To me, this is success in its truest sense, for of what value is success in any other form, if it does not bring with it a state of true happiness? Please understand—I am not knocking material gains or intellectual achievements. I welcome these like everyone else, but only when they can be mine as a complement to my basic values of love, family, peace of mind, and the ability to live in harmony with myself and others. If I could have my fundamental values together with the other trimmings, the situation naturally would be ideal, but I can be very happy with just my basics alone—with money, position or intellectual accomplishments alone, I can't.

Many times, thinking of how I feel, I have asked myself, "Why me? Why do I feel so great, and yet so many people feel miserable?" When I analyze, I realize that many others have much the same as I, and sometimes even more. Yet many of them are unhappy while I am happy. I am happy with myself, with my marriage, with my family, with my friends, with life. I would not change my life with that of anyone else. I feel loved, liked, respected. Everything seems to come easy for me. I am healthy and energetic, enthusiastic, and I have a constant desire to do things. Every minute of my day is filled with ideas, dreams and projects. Some are small and perhaps insignificant, but I still give them the same enthusiasm I would a trip around the world. I have faith in humanity, trust people in their majority, and count my blessings with each breath of life because God has been so good to me.

Pondering deeper into my state of happiness, I feel certain this beautiful feeling is mine because of a series of attitudes I have gradually developed with the Lord's help. None of these are complex or impossible to achieve. Just as I have done, so can you. The way to happiness I have learned can be yours also if you just dare give it an earnest try.

To prepare ourselves for happiness, we must first acknowledge that we are all born with certain innate and inherent traits and our very own personal emotional makeup which makes each of us different from the other. Next, we must also recognize that our parents, with their tremendous influence over us as babies and children, contributed greatly to making us what we are as adults. The good parents through love, care, understanding, and discipline, did much towards making us happy and well adjusted adult. Some parents may have encountered a tougher job if the child's natural personality characteristics were not the most desirable. There is no question that parents played a very decisive role in shaping us, but whatever undesirable effects they may have had on us are now ours to correct. We must learn to overcome these problems ourselves through self-improvement.

We cannot deny that most of us have hang-ups and personality problems in some form or another, to a lesser or greater degree. Even under the most favorable circumstances in which we may have been fortunate and blessed with good parents, parents themselves are only imperfect human beings who cannot be expected to be infallible. Besides, there are those natural inherent traits and makeup with which we came into this world. So, all of us need to work at self-therapy to a varying extent, depending primarily on these two major factors: our natural traits and our childhood formation.

Feeling sorry for ourselves and blaming our parents is not going to get the job done. Only we can tackle this task, and only we can teach ourselves to be happy through change, and it can be done. Some people may have more complex problems and may need help beyond self-therapy requiring professional guidance to get them started on the road to self-improvement. However, most of us can do the job ourselves through behavior modification and actually changing. In all cases, we should always start the way to happiness armed with the spiritual strength that comes from enlisting help from God through prayer.

We must accept that change is never easy, but we must also acknowledge that change is possible and that if this change can bring us the reward of happy living, it is worth all our efforts and auto-discipline. We should strive to make as total a change as possible in those areas where change is needed, but even when we are unable to accomplish complete change, we should not dismay. Whatever improvement we can achieve represents success and will propel us to continue trying for more.

I know that most persons can find my way to happiness as I have charted in this book if there is willingness and determination to work at improving and perhaps even mastering the same attitudes and principles on which I have been working for years. Some of these attitudes do not come naturally to everyone. Some may be more akin to your nature than others and thus easier to master. I do not believe any one person can cultivate all of these attitudes and principles without putting forth deliberate efforts to change themselves into a happier life.

My very personal recommendation to help make the job easier is to establish a close rapport with God to provide the faith and spiritual strength needed along the way. I realize this is difficult to understand or believe for those who have been living without God. I am also aware that the faith I am professing has to be sought and acquired slowly by experimenting on your own. Through prayer and meditation you will be able to reach the degree of faith needed to overcome the negative attitudes that have been preventing you from happiness. I can only encourage you to seek God as you would a doctor, a psychiatrist, a counselor, a friend, and talk to Him in plain language at your own level. Pour on Him all of your worries and anxieties, with complete belief that He is listening. If you do, I think it will not be too long before you will see clear results which will cause your faith to grow.

As your faith grows, you will watch your life commence to change, slowly at first but quite noticeably, as you start to develop, cultivate, implement, and sometimes even master the following attitudes and principles on which I will subsequently elaborate:

1. Love yourself without feelings of guilt.
2. Find happiness in giving happiness.
3. Practice the Golden Rule of doing unto others as you would them do unto you, with tolerance and kindness.
4. Give of yourself to others so that you too can receive from them.
5. Take off those fighting gloves and stop acting on the defensive constantly.
6. Count your blessings and learn to find joy in the many small things life offers.
7. Plan and work to make your dreams come true.
8. Keep enthusiasm, optimism and positive attitudes in your life.
9. Don't demand perfection of yourself or others.
10. Keep busy and productive.
11. Learn to say "I'm sorry."
12. Don't be super sensitive.
13. Control your temper and keep your cool.
14. Put things in their proper perspective.
15. Live today. Don't sacrifice it worrying about tomorrow and regretting yesterday.
16. Accept that life presents problems at times. Rap with God, face them and bounce back.
17. Keep young at heart as you up in years.
18. Be willing to change whatever attitude that may be causing you unhappiness, realizing change is never easy and rarely

total or instant, but always possible to some extent if you are willing to work at it.

I am aware the world has changed and that there are many new kinds of marital arrangements which I respect because they share that all important ingredient: love. I am not judging these new relationships, but I believe I do not need to apologize for favoring and advocating traditional marriage between a man and a woman, as intended by God.

Despite the changes that have occurred in our world, I cannot emphasize enough that seeking and finding happiness is important for everyone, and it is achievable for everyone. I hope that all readers, regardless of their sexual orientation, will strive to find this elusive feeling of happiness by tenaciously following the principles discussed in this book.

Because I am a woman that loves being a woman, with admiration for men and the beautiful difference that exists between us, I have dedicated a chapter especially to women and men and their challenging roles. I have also dedicated a chapter to working women whether with a regular job, career or in business, and very especially to wives who are mothers and their husbands or mates, as well as to single mothers.

My hope is that my message may reach everyone in their different roles who have not yet found lasting happiness. I sincerely desire that my words will inspire them to reach this beautiful spiritual feeling called happiness through the principles that I have elaborated in this book.

CHAPTER 1

Don't Feel Guilty About Loving Yourself

According to Dr. Hans Selye, a Canadian doctor who is a world famous expert on stress, if we are to be healthy and happy, we must of necessity think of ourselves first and all others in relation to what they can do to contribute to our well being. This may appear to be a very selfish approach to life, contrary to what most of us have been taught. Nonetheless, scientists have proven that egotism is a law of nature which cannot be disobeyed without paying for it in the form of stress in some manner or other. Unselfishness as taught to us is in violation of every normal biological rule. We deceive ourselves into thinking it is wrong to think of our interest first, and then feel guilty when we cannot help but feel that way. However, this natural concept that cannot be denied does not mean that uncontrolled selfishness should be encouraged to the point that you do not care what you do to others as long as you get your way. Such an extreme attitude is certainly not recommendable and ultimately will result in unhappiness to you.

Dr. Selye states we should try to cultivate a type of selfishness which he calls "altruistic egotism." In other words, by being useful to someone, there is advantage to be gained by you so that instead of doing good just because you love your neighbors, you should also do good so your neighbors will love you. It is really a simple and natural philosophy. By doing good to others, you feel good, and your inner self feels satisfied with your actions while at the same time you are bringing about good to others. The motivation is selfish, but the end results bring benefits to both you and the other person.

If you learn to master altruistic egotism, you can rid yourselves of harmful stress. Beneficial stress is necessary to live, but harmful stress or distress can be the cause of psychosomatic illnesses as well as other tension-caused sicknesses as heart attacks, gastric ulcers, migraine headaches, upset stomach, etc. Dr. Selye indicates that each of us has only a certain amount of adaptation energy which gives us the ability to cope with stress. If we exhaust this supply of adaptation energy, we can become sick and develop tension diseases. Altruistic egotism channels our normal selfish instincts in a productive way so they become beneficial to others as well. You should earn the love and respect of others, creating in them a natural desire for your own well being. The results will be beneficial to all. Altruistic egotism as a way of life can only be to the advantage of society as a whole.

It is to your benefit and well being to create fewer problems for yourselves in all of your relationships —- with husbands, children, friends, bosses, co-workers, parents, in-laws, etc. In the process, you create fewer problems for them as well. You must learn to relate to people. Unpleasant relations can cause great tension when bickering, arguments and hostility prevail. How much simpler it would be if everyone were to practice altruistic egotism, creating good will for yourselves with others while at the same time others are creating good will for themselves with you. The results would inevitably be good will for both parties with happier relationships that contribute to your own happiness.

I have lived by this principle for many years much before reading Dr. Selye's s article on altruistic selfishness. My philosophy for many years has been to live harmoniously with myself and others; I just did not know that my philosophy had a name. Long before ever hearing about altruistic egotism, I was applying altruistic egotism in my life not knowing what it was called. In our goal for harmonious living, which is a prime ingredient in achieving happiness, it is very important to remove obstacles from your lives so that living can be smoother and happier. Oddly, it seems as if some people deliberately create obstacles for themselves. By removing these interfering obstacles you are opening the path for happiness.

Here are some real-life examples of how applying my version of altruistic egotism added to my happiness as I removed obstacles which made possible achieving harmony for me and others in various important relationships .

My work has invariably involved working very close with others. Usually, this can be problematic with jealous and competitive feelings developing, especially when two women report to the same man, have equal rank, and have to sit in the same office eight hours each day. I have worked under these conditions in three separate instances and can honestly say that the relationships have worked out well, with true friendship created in each case. I was able to accomplish this by removing the obstacles that were in the way affecting my happiness and that of others.

The first such working relationship took place when I was 21 and had been working only one year for the company with which I completed 30 years of service. Because the secretary of the company's top man had been abruptly taken seriously ill, I was unexpectedly assigned at my very young age to this important position while she recuperated. I loved every minute of the new job because the person with whom I worked was such a kind, fair, and intelligent person, and my work was very interesting. After four months, she returned, not fully recovered and I was asked to continue assisting her until she could handle the job alone.

My problems began when I realized that this lady, about 30 years my senior, was very zealous of her job, extremely temperamental, and saw in me a genuine threat as a younger woman. She did not take much time in letting me feel her dislike and lack of trust. For a few days I felt totally miserable. What to do? I saw no alternative but to make things better for myself and realized I had to adopt an attitude that would make the unpleasant situation tolerable for me. With this as a goal, my natural instinct told me that I needed to remove the obstacles that were causing me problems. I began by concentrating on doing my work as efficiently as possible. I did not allow her actions to unduly bother me because I was able to understand that she was acting out of insecurity and fear. This reasoning motivated me to do all possible to have her see clearly that I had no intention to displace her which was the major obstacle that was upsetting the relationship. First, I resorted to taking an impersonal attitude, not only to shelter myself, but also with the hope that by showing disinterest, my actions would prove to her that I was not a threat. I went about my business diligently, did exactly what was asked of me, and kept out of her way as much as possible. Never pushing myself in any way, I paid little attention to any pettiness that could upset me. This plan of action paid off for in less than a month, this lady became intrigued at my lack of interest in competing for the position and began taking me into her confidence. I was gradually able to win her respect and trust through my behavior and sincerity. As I gained her good will, she opened up more and grew warmer until I became like a daughter to her.

Since she never recovered totally, I continued working with her permanently and became her young protégé. We both benefited from the association, and the relationship, which began out of mutual necessity, evolved into real friendship, with many pleasant memories created during those years. If I had not removed the obstacles in the relationship, this happy ending would not have happened. We worked jointly as secretaries to the same man for several years until she became a victim of cancer. At that time, she insisted with our boss that I should be the person to take her place demonstrating she had genuine love for me as I had for her. This is a beautiful story which could have ended differently if I had not practiced altruistic egotism to our mutual benefit.

My second such close working relationship was much easier. I cannot take credit entirely for the wonderful relationship that ensued because the woman with whom I worked for over ten years was such a wonderful and likeable person that it was only natural to establish a beautiful relationship. I believe both of us unknowingly practiced altruistic egotism. We never felt threatened one by the other, nor did either ever try to outdo the other. Instead, we helped each other, shared, laughed together, and created a lasting friendship through the years which brought us both much happiness.

The third such close working arrangement lasted for almost ten years also. However, she was not as easygoing and uncomplicated as my friend before her. In fact, she herself confessed that she had a problem getting along with people because she had little patience, practically no tolerance, had insecurity issues, and lost her cool easily.

Quite a menu for me to face. At the onset, fearing what was ahead, I recognized that I needed to win her confidence by having her see me as a friend and not a competitor. It was vital that I prove to her that she need not be on the defensive with me and that we could work out any problems with sincerity without losing our cool. Of course, this was far from easy.

However, using common sense people skill, I was able to impress her with the fact that I was just trying to make life as pleasant as possible for myself and for her in the relationship. Targeting her insecurity issues, I convinced her that in no way I wished to compete or create problems for her. Since my actions supported my sincerity, it became evident to her that I was a fair person that could be trusted. By gaining her trust, I was able to remove an important obstacle that was blocking the relationship. I did everything possible to show her I considered her intelligent and capable which I realized meant a great deal to her. In time, she became aware we could be friends to our mutual benefit. In the course of the years we worked together, we did become friends and removed conflicts from our working day. I earned her good will for my own selfish interest, but in so doing, created a pleasant relationship which she also enjoyed.

After Jay and I had been married for two years, for various compelling reasons, we decided to move to Havana. At 20, this was a big change for me that involved leaving my country and my family. At first, while we got settled and on our own, we lived with his parents. This temporary arrangement lasted six years until we built our home and were able to move away. His parents were good people, but quite different from my own family. They were very old-fashioned, and just completely different from me in their ways. Saving money meant a great deal to my father-in-law, and they lived a very frugal life, looking with displeasure at our more liberal spending ways. There were many differences as are apt to be when people of different backgrounds and age attempt to live together.

Again, I saw my alternatives. We could either move or become independent, or if, for reasons of interest to us, we chose to stay together, I had to learn to live in this different setup. My mission was to win their love and good will, and make our life and theirs as happy as possible. The fact that we were living in their house which was their domain aggravated the situation. I could have done much better if they had been living with us, but since the reverse was true, more sacrifice was needed on my part.

With sincerity, love, and intelligent behavior, I won their love. By injecting enthusiasm into their lives, I brought a new kind of joy to their rather dull lives, and they took me in as their daughter. We lived in harmony for six yeas with very little friction. Perhaps, I would have found this situation much more difficult if I had thought the arrangement was permanent, but under the circumstances, I made those six years as happy as possible for myself, for them and for my husband.

In one of my most important jobs when we moved to Miami, I was challenged to work with a most difficult person. This relationship was different because this time, I was faced with a despotic boss and not a coworker. The situation meant that if I did not overcome, I could lose my important position or even worse, my job with the company. I had to handle the relationship in such a way as to create minimal problems for myself, and at the same time prove my capability. In my mind I had a simple choice with two options. Either I quit or learned to cope. The first was out of the question from a selfish point of view since I had invested 9 years with the firm, had a salary not easily attainable elsewhere with many fringe benefits, and enjoyed the work. For these reasons, I was not about to throw away so much because of one difficult person. Therefore, I opted to learn to work with him so that those eight hours each day would be less stressful and more pleasant for me. Much easier said than done, of course.

Initially, I handled the relationship as impersonally as possible to protect myself from getting hurt, reasoning that he had employed me for my services and assistance, and I had accepted the position for the salary and other benefits. At first, this was exactly how I evaluated the relationship. I did not expect more from him nor did I intend to give him more than what I was contracted to do. With this attitude, I thought I could function with aloofness and self-confidence, and he could not reach me. But, I needed to remove the primary obstacle before anything else. This required my impressing him that I was not intimidated by his "bully" style and that I was entirely sure of my ability to deliver what he needed. As I showed that I did not fear his behavior and was quite capable in my work, he began to ease on his style. This strategy was the key to my initial success, and gradually I won the battle through various ways that I learned as I encountered each obstacle.

As I did, sincere affection developed between us during the twelve years we worked together. By successfully coping with the difficult association for my own selfish reasons, I had also made this man's life happier when he was able to enjoy a more personal rapport with his secretary as a person whom he had grown to like and respect. This warmer and more civil relationship certainly was much better for him also rather than working with an aloof and indifferent person. My one-time difficult boss became a lasting and good friend.

Out of a natural desire to remove obstacles, before I knew the altruistic egotism principle existed, I applied it in my marriage many times and always with good results. My husband has always wanted to do things for me and to please me. Yet, I never have demanded. I have always been soft-spoken by nature, and learned early in the marriage that Jay reacted favorably, as most people, to affectionate requests rather than domineering defiant demands. Thus, we both benefited because he would have found it impossible to live with a loud-mouthed tyrant, and I would have gotten nowhere except to divorce court. As it is, we have completed 66 years of a wonderful marriage, and my husband is always reassuring me of his love with words and action. When I hear complaints about difficult husbands, and I am told I was lucky to have found such a good man, I know it was not just luck. With God's help I was able to successfully apply my version of altruistic egotism to our marriage creating happiness for both my husband and me.

There are many similar ways in which you can put your selfish motivation to work with beneficial results for you and others as well. If you can learn to live implementing this philosophy, pleasant living could be a reality in most cases, with less effort and tension. You don't have to save altruistic egotism just for the important relationships. It can be used with everyday associations and with everyone with whom you come in contact. It works wonders with sales people at the stores, or any time you are requesting anything from someone.

You will see how much easier life becomes and how people will love to do things for you—almost like magic. You will feel so good deep inside as people react with kindness and pleasantries while at the same time you are also making people feel great as you win their good will. A warm smile, a thank you, a sincere please, that soft tone in your voice, all of these things, small as they may seem, work miracles in removing obstacles from your life and creating a less stressful and more pleasant life for you. Is this not what you and everyone else are seeking?

RULE 1: LOVE YOURSELF, CREATE LESS PROBLEMS FOR YOURSELF BY REMOVING OBSTACLES FROM YOUR LIFE LIVING BY THE ALTRUISTIC EGOTISM PRINCIPLE.

CHAPTER 2

Find Happiness In Giving Happiness

Since we must all love ourselves first, and there is no doubt this is a natural and normal condition, we should not apologize nor feel guilty for being motivated by our selfish desire to feel good. However, would it not be wonderful if we could all channel this basic force so that while we are making ourselves happy, the effect will also produce happiness for others? Just look at it this way.

If my selfish interest in feeling good can be satisfied by seeing my husband happy and content when he goes off to play golf, I will have obtained satisfaction not only for myself, but will have also made my husband a happy man. If my selfish interest to feel good can be fulfilled with the happiness I see in my children's face when I offer help by lending our van when they have needed a larger car for moving purposes, I would have made them happy also. Or if by providing storage room in our house to our children because we have more space made them happy, I would have also made myself happy. In each case, I was able to find happiness by giving happiness. This principle can be applied to many aspects of your everyday living.

There have been many times when I have felt great happiness when I have caused others to be happy or when I have watched others being happy. I can remember years ago, doing housework, which I don't really cherish, in the midst of scrubbing my tub, my thoughts wandered to my family. As I visualized my older daughter happy with her husband and their own projects, and my teenager with her record player turned on full blast, right then and there, kneeling at that tub, I was a very happy woman because I knew my loved ones were happy. Although at that particular moment I was not doing what I liked best, I was capable of experiencing happiness through their happiness. I have had these moments many times through the years when I have had that wonderful feeling of happiness just by knowing that someone was happy. Perhaps, during those moments I was not doing something especially pleasant or that was on my list of favorite things, but I was able to feel happiness through their happiness.

I have always made a big fuss over Christmas and have received much happiness in getting everyone the things I knew they wanted. I have spent hours planning, scheming and shopping for everyone and have derived joy just thinking of how happy they would be when they opened the gifts. It is so much fun to see people truly happy because of something you have done. You can receive almost infinite happiness this way, and this is a very good way of channeling your natural selfishness. Giving to your loved ones makes you happy, and receiving the things they wanted makes them happy. It's a two-way street.

Life is a series of gives and takes. There are many ways in our lives to cause happiness in others, at the same time creating happiness for ourselves. When you cook someone's favorite dish, you can sense a good feeling of accomplishment and pride in yourself; when you buy your children or your grandchildren whatever they have been wanting even though you may have had to put off getting something you wanted, you can enjoy a sense of happiness for being such a good and magnanimous parent or grandparent. You can feel quite good for being a considerate wife or mate, when you watch over your tired partner's sleep or when you take over one of your overworked partner's chores. The list can go on and on limited only by your imagination and ability to find happiness by making someone else happy. There are many similar sources of happiness in everyone's life which can produce happiness for others, if you allow them to be. Here are some that I have experienced:

    I recall when my daughter Adele was pregnant, and the summer heat in her non-air conditioned car made her sick driving to and from work, I quickly let her borrow my car for an indefinite length of time. Not once did I feel victimized or miserable because of what I had given up. I was happy to provide this relief for her. On another occasion, when the opportunity came up for my mother to take a fantastic trip around South America, it would not have been possible unless I could fill in for her in taking care of our grandson. I did not have to be asked. I promptly offered to dedicate part of my vacation time to cover for her. It made me very happy to make possible this well deserved break for my mother who was always doing things for us.

    I am one of those baby sitters who never had to be approached tactfully or with fear of a negative or of accepting reluctantly. I received tremendous joy when I saw my daughter and son taking off happily for an evening together that I had made possible, and of course, at the same time, I was ecstatic over having precious time with my grandson. One summer when my daughter Annette was on school vacation, I set aside two days each week against my vacation to happily drive her and friends to the beach. Since she was too young to drive, I came to the rescue knowing she would have been bored all day at home. Every week when I picked her up and her friends and went off to the beach with chaise, cooler, and enough reading material to keep me entertained, I truly thrived watching them having such a great time.

Although I enjoyed sailing to a point, there were times when I would have liked to stay home and do something else. Knowing that Jay really needed me along when he did not have a better First Mate, I happily accompanied him. I experienced much happiness as I observed his bright smile and happy expressions challenging the wind at times and other times just relaxing in the deep blue. Staying home doing my thing could never have fulfilled me as much as the happiness I received through his happiness.

One great two-way happiness moment occurred when I made the decision to forego changing my car and instead used the funds to present Adele and Stan with a gift towards their down payment on a home they were so hoping to buy. They needed more space with the new baby and his possessions. Without a doubt I could have used a new car, considering I was driving a 1968 Pontiac in 1977. However, if my old car could provide transportation for me adequately for one more year, I could save the money and present it to them as our gift towards the new house. They had not asked us for help nor did they expect it, but if my giving up on a new car allowed me the pleasure of giving them this help, it was well worth the sacrifice.

Years after, when Adele and Stan had been married for over 20 years, Jay and I won two first class tickets on American Airlines to anywhere in Europe. Immediately, both of us thought of them because Stan had never been able to travel much and had always wanted to visit Germany and seek his father's roots. We had done so much traveling that one more trip to Europe would not have made a major difference in our lives. Our decision was immediate because Jay also has a natural knack for practicing altruistic egotism. Without further thought, we presented them with the tickets, together with our time share time in Italy. They took off, found Stan's family in Alsace Lorraine, and had the time of their lives. Listening to their excitement over the phone and enjoying their stories when they returned gave us happiness beyond description.

When my grandsons came home permanently from college, they were not financially ready to be on their own. Since their parents were living abroad, we immediately and spontaneously opened our home to them. We created the space and with much love shared their activities with them so they could feel welcome. BJ was a DJ at the time with so much sound equipment that to this day we don't know how we managed, but we did. We enjoyed their poker and barbecue parties in our backyard swarmed with their friends who to this day call us Grandma and Grandpa. Having them with us was so much fun, and they added to our happiness as we did to theirs. The love and joy we received in sharing their lives and happiness cannot be explained with just words. The feeling was really sublime.

Not too long ago, my grandson Ryan, wife Patty and two boys, ages five and three at the time, needed living quarters while their house was being built. They never had to ask. Grandma and Grandpa's house was ready to take them in. We enjoyed them so much, and they were a true source of happiness.

Presently, we are getting injections of happiness in our older years by sharing our home with our daughter Adele and son Stan to make possible their move from Chicago to be closer to their children and grandchildren. Their happiness is providing us with much happiness also.

I do not want to leave the impression that I am a masochist who gets my kicks only from sacrifices or doing things for others. Not so. I am very capable of enjoying things I do for myself also, live a good life of my own, buy things for myself as well, and we have taken many trips of our own. I probably might not have been spurred to do things for just sheer pleasure for undeserving or inconsiderate people or for anyone attempting to take advantage of me. But, for people I love and who deserve anything I can do for them, I am capable of experiencing much happiness by making possible their happiness even at some sacrifice for me.

This is possibly one of the most difficult principles to master because our normal selfish streak takes the better of us, and sometimes it is not easy to keep it in control naturally. When you can go a step further and be capable of experiencing happiness by giving happiness—not with a spirit of martyrdom or with hidden resentment—but with true joy, you will have discovered an enormous source of happiness for yourself and others. I believe this attitude only begins to become natural as we mature because it requires a certain degree of maturity to distinguish the fine line between loving yourself without guilt and being able to experience joy by making someone else happy.

Through the years I have worked on this and have made much progress. Now, I am much more capable of giving happiness and receiving it back by merely causing others to be happy. I marvel at the marked change in me as compared to many years ago. The key to receiving happiness by giving happiness lies in awakening the capability of giving and taking without feeling sorry for yourself. When I was young I probably could not have derived as much happiness in this manner, but as I matured and worked at this principle, it became much more natural for me to find happiness by giving happiness. If you can only experience happiness when something good is happening to you, you will have missed out on many other opportunities to be happy simply by giving happiness.

If this principle were applied by everyone, while you are happy making someone else happy, they in turn would also be happy making you happy, and the results would forcibly be happier people. For this reason, I urge you to work on cultivating it, slowly perhaps, but do not give up on it. Put to work that normal selfish instinct we all have not only for you but for others as well. You will add many happy moments to your life.

RULE 2: LEARN TO EXPERIENCE HAPPINESS BY GIVING HAPPINESS.

CHAPTER 3

Do Unto Others

The Golden Rule may be old and much repeated, but it never becomes outdated because it advocates a simple philosophy which describes human nature itself'. Whether in times bygone or in our day and time, this principle still applies. Think of all the human qualities you appreciate and admire in others and of all of the nice things you enjoy when bestowed upon you by others. If you can develop these same desirable attributes in yourself and do these same nice things to others, without a doubt, others would like and love you more. It is as uncomplicated as ABC.

If you can do unto others as you would have them do unto you, you would be automatically putting into practice many good principles through this one simple Rule. Here are some very important ones which can contribute much towards making you a happier person and in the process make others happier, too:

Be kind and compassionate.
Through kindness, such as you yourself appreciate from others, be compassionate with others You should allow others to save face just as you appreciate

when someone has not embarrassed you or not hit you when you were already down. Practicing kindness with others will remove cruelty and meanness from your life which are bad and negative feelings that you should cast out.

Be forgiving.
Everyone will need to be forgiven at some time in life. No one is so infallible that this need will not come up at some point. Old grudges are usually remembered only by the person who holds them and lives with the destructive feeling. The person who is target of hatred is not as affected as the person who does the hating. When it is your turn to be forgiven, and that moment will occur, it is good to know that people can forgive and forget. Practice forgiveness and you will feel immense relief as you are able to put aside resentment and ill feelings. Forgiveness is both beautiful and necessary.

Be tolerant of others.
Realizing how great you feel when others accept you, do the same for others by accepting their differences in personality, culture, intelligence, education, race, nationality, religion, age, sex orientation, etc. Regardless of differences, we all have in common certain human qualities which are much the same in all of us. Tolerating and accepting persons whom you do not like just because they are so different from you is necessary even if you cannot understand them.

This is especially true if you stop to consider that they may feel the same way about you. If everyone were to practice the Golden Rule, tolerating and accepting each other, how much more happiness would be bred for all. This does not mean you will become best friends with everyone, although it could happen if given a chance. We know there will be people you will like more than others, and it is your privilege to choose with whom you prefer to associate, but this prerogative does not give you the right to hurt or to be disrespectful to those you do not like. This is particularly true if the dislike is provoked merely by people's different customs or appearances and not by something they have done. You should remember that no one can feel so high and superior that he or she may not be considered different also by someone else.

The problem of discrimination and intolerance of others is a matter of point of view. If you could temporarily become the person you cannot tolerate or that you discriminate against, you would probably be shocked to discover how that person views you. For instance, if you were to become Jewish for a few days, or a black or Asian person, you would be astonished to find that they also have their own opinions about your kind. Each kind tends to discriminate, and yet each is also a target of discrimination. Basically, each can be the discriminator and the object of discrimination, dependent only on point of view.

The following actual stories demonstrate how people can perceive others erroneously without being aware they are also being perceived incorrectly by those they are discriminating against.

Having both Hispanics and non-Hispanics friends and acquaintances, I have heard erroneous opinions from both sides. Some of my Hispanic friends have expressed themselves in a very derogatory manner about non-Hispanic women branding them as poor mothers and considering them of low morals and with poor cleanliness habits. Ironically, I have heard some of my non Hispanic friends apologetically express themselves poorly of Hispanic women. They consider them to have loose morals merely because they appeared to them less inhibited and more sensuous. They also believe they were poor disciplinarians of their children. Oddly, neither suspected how they were being viewed by the other side.

I had never heard the expression "Cuban baths," and was surprised to learn that many non-Hispanics describe a "Cuban bath" to be a quick wash-up without taking an actual bath which would imply they believe that Cubans do not bathe regularly. Of course, this is an erroneous concept since I knew that Cubans in general consider a daily bath as an absolute must. However, what I found humorous was that I was aware that on the other side there was the impression that non-Cubans did not bathe daily. And, I also knew that many Cuban women found it difficult to understand how non-Cuban women could function without using a bidet and manage to keep fresh between baths. Cuban women generally were accustomed to using bidets in their homes for more thorough feminine hygiene. In fact, this practice has produced such a demand in Miami that a portable version of bidet that can be installed on toilets is readily available in many plumbing fixture stores.

These stories are not only humorous but depict clearly how persons can erroneously see others without realizing that they too are being viewed erroneously by others.

The world is made of different kinds, and people of different backgrounds will always appear different and sometimes wrong to others. It is important to realize that no matter how right you may think you are, others may see you differently so go easy when you catch yourself not being tolerant. Remember no one is immune to being the target of discrimination.

Genuinely like and trust people, giving of yourself to others.
You enjoy being treated warmly and affectionately, so you should respond to others similarly. Everyone needs to be liked and accepted, but so many people are afraid to give of themselves for fear of getting

hurt. Distrusting humanity, they go around alienating themselves and shielding themselves from love and affection by keeping at a cautious distance. Then they wonder why they do not get more out of their relationships. You must give of yourself in order to receive. If you are incapable of showing true interest in people, they will respond to you in the same way. As long as you keep an aloof attitude, you may not get hurt, but you will receive very little from others, and that's a very sterile way of living. You must be willing to risk getting hurt and to give friendship and show affection if you wish to have friends and to have people take you in. It is just a gamble. If you happen to lose at times, the risk was certainly worthwhile for the many times you will come up on top. We cannot develop enthusiasm for people who show apathy in relating to others to avoid getting hurt. So, get involved with people and let go of your fear.

Trust is key for liking people and having them respond to you. You appreciate when others show they trust you. In like manner, you should trust others until you have factual reasons to not do so, in which case you will probably not care to cultivate their friendship anyway. This can happen occasionally, but it should not deter you from trusting people initially. People are generally good, if we give them a chance. Everyone is not going to be your true blue friend. You can only have a few of these during a lifetime, but certainly you can make many pleasant acquaintances, if you dare trust people in general. Many casual acquaintances can become good friends, if we treat them with trust and sincere warmth.

Do not be indiscreet and pry into other people's lives.

Just as you treasure your right to privacy and dislike when someone tampers with it and meddles in your business, so should you respect this same right in others. Do not ask indiscreet questions. Let people tell you what they wish to tell you and no more. Unsolicited advice or unrequested so-called "constructive criticism" should never be offered. Save this type of counseling for your children or for someone you may be tutoring. Acquaintances and friends do not appreciate this kind of involvement unless specifically requested.

Take off those fighting gloves and stop acting on the defensive.

It is so nice to deal with people that are easy-going and reasonable and can be talked to without fear of immediate rebuttal. You enjoy these desirable characteristics in others, so try your best to react similarly with others. You should not go around life always on the defensive pouncing back as if you were under constant attack by the world at large. If you see in everyone a possible enemy or competitor, you are making life miserable for yourself because that kind of attitude simply does not lend itself to creating friendship or making people fond of you. Just as you shy away from the type of person who is always ready to fight, others will feel the same about you. Don't lose your cool and keep those fighting gloves off until you may really need to defend yourself.

Be presto to recognize and accept your mistakes. Think of the kind of reaction you would like to receive if you were pointing out an error to someone. You would want the person to accept the error intelligently and not defiantly. Then, when it is your mistake that is being signaled out, do not react defensively but react in the exact same manner that you like others to react to you.

You should be quick to accept errors and not feel that admitting a mistake reflects on your intelligence or capabilities. Quite contrary, it takes an intelligent person to recognize mistakes and to have the humility to admit them. Naturally, if the mistake was not yours, you should calmly and respectfully defend yourself with facts. Again, most people will listen and recognize truth when it is exposed sincerely, correctly and without hysteria.

We will all make mistakes at times. Whenever you err, you must be sincere about admitting and apologizing. Most people will react in an understanding way, and you should not worry about insecure and petty people who cannot get themselves to understand that we are all subject to unintentional human error. These persons are to be pitied for their confused state of mind which will never allow them to be happy unless they change.

As you can see, there are many important ways of applying this old and wise Rule to improve your relationships and to help make you a better and happier person. I have only touched on some, but I am sure you can think of many more, simply by guiding your actions and reactions to those that you enjoy from others.

RULE 3: DO UNTO OTHERS AS YOU WOULD HAVE THEM DO UNTO YOU. BE KIND, COMPASSIONATE, TOLERANT, FORGIVING. GENUINELY LIKE AND TRUST PEOPLE.

CHAPTER 4

Just Look Around You

We should learn to appreciate everything, small as any may be. Usually the things that can bring us most joy are right in front of us, but so many times we search far and wide for them without realizing this. You can derive joy from a plant in bloom, a beautiful sunset, a lovely song .You can get a charge from trying a new recipe, getting a new haircut, and you can experience some very happy moments from snuggling in a cozy chair to read a good book. The big moments in life are few and far between. If we save the great feeling of joy just for these, we will have wasted much precious living and time just waiting. How many times we yearn and look for those big kicks we are certain exist in other people's lives, not ours, only to find when we really get up close, they actually did not exist at all. Oftentimes, we discover that the people we so much admired were not as happy as we thought. Do not pass by the many sources of happiness within your reach looking for those outside your realm which may not make you as happy as you think if you found them. Remember the grass is not always greener on the other side. When you get up close, there can be a lot of chinch bug.

We all have many blessings —- recognizing them is what is difficult sometimes. But, when you have acquired this ability and have learned to be happy with just about every pleasant thing around you, you will see how much more beautiful life can be. Most of us do not need to be blessed with more—all we need is to cultivate the ability to recognize the blessings we already have. Once we can achieve this, we have plugged in the light to a whole new world and life for us.

Before retirement, getting up and getting started each weekday was difficult for me primarily because I loved my home and family. Although I enjoyed work once there, I hated to part with my personal life each morning. It did not take long for me to overcome the negative feeling. As soon as I saw a beautiful plant that hung in the bathroom, and if I was so fortunate to find it had a bloom as it often did, I would start feeling good inside. Then the thought of breakfast enthused me. Jay and I would sit together outside in our patio for a short breakfast each morning, looking at the fresh moist grass, the thriving plants hanging all around, and hearing the lively chirp of the many birds about us. I was completely awakened to the beautiful world with which God has blessed us, and I was ready to face the day after all.

If I had not tried to find these small things, I would have stumbled about, upset with having to go to work, and would have started the day on a sour note. I would have driven off into the morning traffic in a negative mood, and each successive problem would have appeared more and more insurmountable. Instead, by the time I was driving to work, battling the traffic, I was full of pleasant thoughts of how good it was to be alive and healthy and how great it was to have peace of mind and a good job. And these positive thoughts got me started on plans for weekend activities. I toyed with the idea of whether we would barbecue and invite some special friends, or perhaps there was a good movie to watch, and my mind ran on and on with any number of pleasant thoughts. By the time I reached the office, even traffic appeared rather good that morning. And that can take a bit of positive thinking.

Through the years I have learned to enjoy many things. I have found a way of my own to derive joy from every good thing around me. Hardly a day goes by that I do not have at least one small reason or happening to add spark to my day. These are usually very insignificant, by most people standards, but to me they are big enough to provide the additional oomph to what would be a routine day. Sometimes, it may be new photos in the camera ready to be downloaded or rearranging furniture, listening to a new record, eating a good orange or some other fruit in season that I like, planning what I will wear for a special occasion that is coming up, changing a flower arrangement, or shifting my plants from one area to another to create a different look in the house. I enjoy playing with our dog. I love sitting alone and observing the various items that we have collected during trips. At times when everyone is asleep I enjoy the solitude sitting in my living room or family room with a great feeling that everything is just the way I like it. I can feel like a million dollars with a new dress or a pair of shoes. And, it is great to sit in the evenings with Jay holding hands, just quietly relaxing exchanging a word here and there and thanking God for our blessings. This quiet but warm closeness that is experienced by two people in love can bring much joy. The kiss my husband gives me sometimes when he stands behind me as I am in the kitchen can make me as happy as a trip around the world. I can find joy even in grocery shopping as I stack up all the goodies in the cart with a surprise for Jay, goodies for the great grandchildren and a treat for myself. All of these things, and many more, can make me look forward to a very ordinary day with enthusiasm.

Count your blessings. Believe me, you are so lucky! When you become capable of recognizing them, you will have tapped on a limitless source of happiness which will make you feel good every day. If you are healthy and self-sufficient, you already have more blessings than you can ever be thankful for. I am sure everyone can come up with an extensive list of blessings—all as different as we are in our likes and dislikes. Make that list, and you will be surprised to find how many pleasant small things exist, and some not so small, within your reach if you learn to recognize them.

RULE 4: COUNT YOUR BLESSINGS AND FIND JOY IN THE SMALL THINGS IN LIFE.

CHAPTER 5

Organize And Act Out Your Dreams

Have you ever wondered why it seems as if some people always have most of their dreams come true? Why is it that some folks get more done and always appear to know what they want and which way they are going? Believe me; these people are not blessed with any special powers or luck. They have simply learned and disciplined themselves to evaluate their dreams realistically, and once convinced the dream was possible and was worth working for, they planned to make it reality. Again, to some, because of their innate nature, this ability comes easier than for others, but this principle, like all others, can be cultivated, and your lives will take a new dimension of achievement and purpose.

Have a plan so you will know which way you are going and how you might get there. Planning is important and is the first step toward converting dreams into real live happenings. It is good to dream and to look forward with anticipation to those things you want, but you must do something more than just dream. Dreaming is the engine starter, but nothing will move if you do not go beyond this stage. You must organize those dreams into a plan that will make them come true. I have known many dreamers who feel very disappointed and discouraged because they never seem to get beyond dreaming. They always blame fate, luck, destiny, and others for not being able to fulfill their dreams—never themselves. Actually, in most cases, they have no one else to blame because they have done nothing to make their dreams come true. If you are a habitual dreamer, with a poor fulfillment record, it is time to change this behavior pattern to one that will give you a sense of accomplishment and will bring you all those things you want so much. It is in your hands, and you alone can do it.

I have found that the best way to start working on a dream is to begin with a plan that you can visualize. First, of course, you must have evaluated the dream as to its possibilities of materializing. You must be realistic about your dreams. You cannot dream of a million dollar mansion if your means are well below that goal. At least, not for a near future. Maybe, as part of a long-range plan, if you are willing to work toward an income that can make such a dream possible, you can have this dream, too. However, you must recognize it will take more time and work than a more reachable dream that can happen in your immediate future. Once you are convinced that your dream is realistically attainable, outline your plan of action and persistently follow it. Expect and be prepared to overcome obstacles along the way. Nothing comes totally easy in life, and making dreams come true is no exception. You cannot expect for dreams to come true just by sheer luck and magic. It takes work, stick-to-itiveness, confidence in yourself and faith that the Lord will guide and help you.

You must always have an alternate plan, a Plan B, in the event the original plan cannot be accomplished exactly as projected. If the alternate plan is the closest to making your dream come true at the present time, accept it with contentment and enjoy it. You can keep working on your original dream if it continues to mean that much to you but rejoice that the alternate has gotten you that much closer to your dream. Now the dream has become tangible and you can almost touch it.

I have always been a planner by nature and have been mocked by family and friends because I make lists for everything. However, I have proven that planning has made me come up on top every time by accomplishing goals that did not appear possible. In this chapter I will illustrate this principle with actual stories so you can vividly see how dreams, as impossible as they may appear at times, can come true if you take the needed steps, and always keep God as a partner.

Our first dream. This was a most important and an almost unreachable dream except for the Lord's miraculous doings. My husband and I met when we were practically children. He was 15 and I was 12. It happened during our family's yearly three-month summer vacation in Cuba spending time with my mother's family. The family lived in a small town very close to Havana where life was simple and good. Everyone knew each other, no crime to speak of, and it was a fun haven for me because I was allowed to enjoy with little restrictions. It is in this kind of setting that one day Jay and I met at the house of friends who lived next to my grandfather. The family with two girls and two boys, all older than I, were wonderful people with a great ability for creating an atmosphere that attracted the young to meet there. One such day, a group of town boys were playing cards; the girls were busy at girl talk, when a torrential summer shower came upon us. No one could leave for hours. Without a doubt, the Lord had a plan for us. He led me to play piano to while away the time, and a 15-year old boy got up from the card game to listen. We talked for hours, forgetting everyone else as if only we existed. He told me he played trumpet in the town band and also played with a small group in local town dances. Music was his thing, and he was fascinated with the new popular American song I was playing: "As Time Goes By" (which became our song forever and ever). This is how our love story began and continued each year during summer vacations.

This love story was highly improbable to ever come to fruition because we were so young, and I lived in the United States and he lived in Cuba. After my departure each year, we kept alive what we had by writing to each other faithfully. Although we saw each other only once a year, impossible as it may appear perhaps in today's world, that young spark grew into love from year to year. There were so many hurdles to jump, but as the years passed we passionately wanted to marry and be together forever. My parents liked him, but they were concerned there was just too much to overcome for our relationship to endure. As parents, they questioned the obvious. How could we get it together? How was Jay going to be able to come to the U.S. legally with all the red tape involved? Even if this could be achieved, what were the possibilities of his getting a job in a new country with a language barrier? What about the million other problems that needed to be solved? Because of our youth, we did not weigh these obstacles. We just believed in our love, continued hoping, planning, fervently praying and never gave up on our dream.

In a most beautiful and miraculous way, the Lord delivered the impossible and began putting the pieces of the puzzle in place until it took shape. At 18 and 21 we married in Tampa, and our beautiful life together began. Now, 66 years later, we look back at how our first dream came true and see clearly the Lord's amazing intervention, coupled with our own desire to remain faithful to each other.

Our second dream: our first car.

Once married, our dream was to have our own car. Today, this may not to appear to be an extraordinary or difficult dream to achieve. But, in 1949, a few years after the end of the war, for a young couple with little income who had just begun getting it together, a new car was indeed an almost impossible dream. We watched this dream shape into reality by planning and by enlisting the Lord's help, as usual. We had little cash, but we were set on getting that new car so we started planning for it. First, we checked into the various makes and determined which car was affordable for us that could fulfill our dream. We decided for a Chevrolet four-door sedan. We figured how much money we would need for the down payment and what kind of monthly payments we could handle. At the time new cars were scarce after the war, and the car dealer warned it would take approximately six months for delivery. We welcomed the waiting time to be able to save for our down payment; we knew we could afford the monthly payments.

Our much desired maroon color Chevy arrived a few months ahead of schedule, and we were minus some money. God sent an angel to the rescue: my Godfather and aunt. As soon as they heard, they gave us the amount we needed, and when we drove off with our new 1950 Chevy, we had made our first dream together as a couple come true. This happened because we had planned, worked and prayed for it and God did the rest.

Our next big dream: our first child. This was a difficult decision for me. We had married so very young and had agreed to wait several years before starting a family. As time got closer, I never found the right time to assume the responsibility. First, we wanted to travel to Europe because I had enticing travel opportunities as an airline employee. We could go to Spain for very little, and this motivated us to start planning for this major trip. Scheduled to leave

March 1952, with vacation time requested, and everything all set for this dream trip, a major upset occurred. A few months before the planned trip, the precise airplane that flew the Havana/Madrid route fell over the Azores with almost a total loss of passengers. I knew the crew intimately because I had been working with the flight crew on a daily basis so I was bereaved and terribly shocked. The Havana/Madrid flight at that time was operated with DC4 equipment and flight time was 24 hours. Since I have never been fond of flying, the 24-hour trip had already made me a bit apprehensive, but this tragic happening aggravated my fear. Just barely two years with the airline, this was my first close-up experience with an accident of this magnitude in which I was so closely involved.

I just could not visualize sitting on a similar plane for 24 hours after this accident. Jay understood but was disappointed. He negotiated: if we don't go to Madrid as planned, we will start looking for our first baby, and take a road trip through the island instead. Fair enough, I thought. I had never been through the entire 1000-mile island and a baby would probably not happen right away, so I accepted. I did not know that God had other plans. During our very interesting road trip, I began noticing symptoms in my body that had me concerned. I was nauseous and feeling different. Surely there had to be something very wrong with me. It was impossible that I could be pregnant so soon. Voilá! On our return, the doctor confirmed I had all of two months.

Once I knew I was going to be a mother, all my previous insecurity of having a baby vanished. Having this new life in me brought me some very precious moments, and seven months later Adele, our first born, came into our lives as a source of a new and unimaginable joy. Again, the Lord had His own plan for us, and He did not make us wait for this dream.

Later, our big dream was a home of our own. After our first two years of marriage living in Tampa, we moved to Havana because Jay had been offered a good job opportunity. Purchasing a home for a couple of youngsters with just jobs but zero cash was not an easy feat. Jay worked with the Cuban Electric Company, and we knew the company offered loans for building purposes to employees through their Retirement Fund with certain caveats. The employee needed to have at least five years with the company and own the land.

As a planner, I recognized that the first step was to buy our land while Jay accumulated those five years. We fell in love with a newly developed beautiful spot, and gradually paid for the land while waiting for the required time. Our dream to build was a topic that we discussed frequently during those five years, and we never gave up on the hope that it would be a reality some day. Since we had little cash, it appeared like just dream talk. But, we were determined, and I knew I would get there if God gave us health and our jobs. The five years passed, our land was paid, and we were ready to act out our dream.

We drew a sketch of our dream house with careful detail. I think we enjoyed this planning stage almost as much as actually living the house later. Next, we needed a qualified architect that would not charge excessively. Again, this was not easy, but I prayed and God delivered. A relative of my mother was a reputable architect, and he immediately took over the project and never charged us a penny. The next step was to find a builder. We checked out various builders and were almost ready to go ahead when a friend with building experience recommended someone whom he knew to be very reliable and honest. We were not too impressed, because he was a ruddy type, void of diplomacy and tact, and called it as it was. Quite frankly and bluntly he told us it was impossible to build a house such as we projected for the money we had. Our bubble was crushed!

This brusque awakening to reality was heartbreaking, but the pain did not last long because we started working on an alternate plan revising the house plans to a more realistic level. We managed to retain as many of the important features as we could but brought down the total square footage. We settled for less, merged areas, designed a very functional bathroom, and the revised layout was a smaller dream house. This time when we presented our new plans to our undiplomatic but honest builder, he told us he could do it. I recall that some of our happiest moments in life were during the time the house was being built. It was a struggle here and there, but as we saw each block go up, we knew our dream was no longer a dream but a real home. We were in awe as we watched our home take shape just as we had planned. It was all that we had envisioned.

Of course, we had to have a plan for furnishing the house while it was being built. Again, money was the problem, as always. We had no credit cards. In 1957 in Cuba they were practically non-existent for the average person. We managed again by planning carefully how much our budget could tolerate. We bought the appliances and air conditioners first, and furnished our living room with simple furnishings. Our bedroom and family room area were done with hand-me-down furniture from my cousin/brother Joe who was leaving for Spain. Between one thing and another, we moved into our new beautiful dream home four months later to the amazement of Jay's parents who never believed we could do it. They had seen us as young irresponsible spenders, but underestimated the power of planning coupled with prayer, optimism, positive thinking, and persistency.

This was another beautiful dream that had come true. Unfortunately, in 1960, for political reasons, we had to leave behind our dream for others to enjoy, but regardless, the joy we experienced in planning, creating and later living this home was exclusively ours to cherish and remember forever.

The dream for freedom. We were confronted with a major problem with the Communist takeover of Cuba. Just one year into this horrendous regime was enough for us to want to leave, but this was a very difficult decision because we had not been directly affected yet. As a young American adult who had never experienced a revolution or seen Communism first hand, I was truly scared. Leaving behind our good jobs, our dream home, and the way of life we had created for ourselves for nine years was not easy. I do not have a gypsy soul and dreaded to leave behind what we had created.

My parents were in the U.S., I was an American living abroad, so returning to my country was much easier than for many already contemplating to leave. I prayed fervently for a solution—with so many thoughts racing through my mind: maybe Castro will be overthrown; our country surely will not allow Communism 90 miles from our shores; maybe something will happen and we will not have to leave. Toward the end of 1959, when the infamous Che Guevara, a communist and murderer, was appointed President of the Cuban National Bank, I approached my North American boss, the PanAm Managing Director in Havana, to discuss our plans. He was very close to the American Ambassador in Havana, and I thought he would be in a better position to forecast the future of the country and that of PanAm. It was my belief that Che's appointment to the National Bank could only mean that PanAm would soon cease operations in Havana because the possibilities that money transfers would be approved were now much more remote. My boss agreed and offered immediately to help by first asking PanAm's Executive Vice President in Miami to approve my transfer to the PanAm Miami Executive Offices with my entire nine years' seniority recognized. He used his influence with the U.S. Embassy to expedite Jay's visa to enter the U.S. as a resident and planned how to get our money out of Cuba. These feats are easily said, but in true life obtaining Jay's resident visa at the Embassy was near to impossible at that time, and getting all our cash out of Cuba was even a greater impossibility. God made both happen. Thus began our steps to exit Cuba.

However, as an optimist, I still hoped and prayed for a solution that would prevent our having to leave. Confusion and indecision reigned. All I could do was to pray and pray for a sign that would give us a clear answer as to whether to leave or not. One evening in December 1959 after pleading desperately to the Lord for clarity in making our decision, I heard a knock at the door. It was dusk, and I was lying down feeling miserable with the effects of wisdom tooth surgery that morning. Jay handled the door, but after a while I became intrigued and tiptoed to take a peek to see who had been at the door and panicked at what I saw. My living room was literally invaded by eight or ten revolutionary militia men and women with machine guns. I had never experienced this kind of terror. They had an order to search our house claiming we were considered dangerous counter revolutionary elements. The search lasted hours, and they went into everything. Their mission was to arrest Jay and take him regardless.

As always, God was with us, and He had other plans. He touched the heart of the group leader who recognized we were just ordinary people who had been unjustly accused and put an end to the search. When they left, at that very moment, without a shred of doubt, I saw clearly the answer to my prayer that evening. The sign I had asked of the Lord could not have been clearer or louder. If this was a preview of what Cuba would become, we did not want any part of it. Suddenly, the jobs, the house, the happy way of life lost total importance.

From that moment forward, the Lord guided us, one step at a time. Three months later we were out of Communist Cuba with our money, with my job at the PanAm Executive Offices approved and my seniority recognized, with Jay's legal U.S. resident visa, and with all of our personal belongings shipped to Miami. Sounds like a miracle? It was! All doors opened for us and closed behind us. It was God's hand in action answering my desperate prayer that evening when I cried out to Him for which path to take. This dream for freedom came true because of our earnest and desperate prayers.

Next, we had a most important dream: our second child before I was 30. Again, I could never find the right moment to have our second baby. I think I always had a subconscious fear of child birth. Adele had been a Caesarean section, and things had been difficult during delivery, so I kept telling myself we should wait. We wanted that second baby but I kept postponing the decision for any number of reasons. God had other plans for us, and Annette came through under the radar, and early 1961, I became pregnant. The biggest and best unplanned blessing bestowed on us, and I give God the credit entirely.

Our first trip to Europe. Now in Miami, after the Havana/Madrid fiasco a few years earlier when we were living in Havana, our dream to travel to Europe remained alive, just waiting for the right moment. Jay was now also with the airlines, and many travel opportunities came our way. However, there are many people in the travel field with similar opportunities who never have done much with their travel privileges although they may have had dreams. We went beyond dreaming and carefully planned our trips, and with God's help, worked to make the dream come true.

Before this trip, we had traveled to closer destinations, but Europe was our big dream. So in 1966 we planned our first trip to Lisbon, Madrid, Paris, and Rome. When we spoke of this major trip, our family never took us seriously. My pessimist mother paid little attention because she knew we were not financially ready for the trip. But, she underestimated us and the power of prayer. With God's help, I had planned how the money could be raised within the time we had to prepare. I wrote hotels, tour operators, and planned airline schedules. We came up with an excellent plan, and we did it! Our first European trip happened with a few scattered insignificant problems which we overcame. We took the entire family including four-year old Annette. When we look back on that first trip, we can only remember the good times. We did it all within the budget and did not waste one minute or one dollar because we had a plan and acted out our plan.

Our second beautiful European family trip took us to Germany, Austria, Italy, and Switzerland in 1970. This trip took much planning because it involved flying to Munich, renting a car and driving from then on. With my usual planning style, I wrote hotels, tour operators, and planned daily mileage to determine our stops. We studied how long we wanted to stay in each place and what we wanted to see and do. I prepared a detailed day to day plan which resulted very workable in actual practice. When we started to work on this dream, Venice and a moonlight gondola ride seemed quite distant, and sometimes even unreachable. Because we planned, tuned God in on our plans, and executed our plan, the dream did come true. This has been true with all of our trips, and we have taken many. All of them were first dreams and talk, later plans and careful preparation, and finally reality with God's help.

The same was true with our trip to Africa, the Orient, Holy Land, the Greek Isles cruise, adding a room and bathroom to the Miami house, and planning our two daughter's weddings within a strict budget. All of these projects were dear dreams that would never have happened if we had not first planned, prayed, and later acted out our dreams.

Our first camping adventure. Jay is an outdoor, practical, former Boy Scout type man—the kind of man with whom you can venture to go camping without fear of being left stranded. Unexpectedly, he was not enthusiastic with the idea of camping when I first approached him with the plan when the girls were 13 and 5. I bought books on camping, wrote to all the Florida State Parks and obtained information on camping facilities. I checked out tent and camping gear rentals and tried to spark an interest in him with stories of some of my friends' terrific camping experiences.

Finally, the girls and I made a dent, and he agreed on our first camping trip. The whole family jointly selected Fort Clinch State Park in North Florida, close to the Georgia Stateline, as the place that had a bit of everything we wanted: beach, woods, trails, plus history all packed into one. My ex-Havana boss loaned us the tent, we rented the cots, and borrowed a lantern. When the day came, we packed everything in boxes into a U-Haul trailer and started our 12-hour drive to Fort Clinch, full of excitement to face this new experience.

Our first problem came just 45 miles into our trip when a tire blew up on the U-Haul trailer. This delayed us and set us back on our schedule so we arrived at Fort Clinch almost with the sunset and only a few minutes of daylight left to set up camp. The second problem arose when the Park Ranger informed us that the park had run out of ice, and we would have to go outside the Park for ice to the town of Fernandina Beach. This would not have been a major problem if I had not bought meat and other perishables just before getting there, and now ice was a must.

Our next problem came up when a big summer shower came upon us. We had no choice but to continue setting up the tent and unpacking. As if this were not enough, the fourth problem appeared when we discovered we had been given the wrong instructions for setting up the tent. There was no way Jay could make the tent stand. Matters were worsened by the strong wind that was blowing on my very romantically selected campsite right by the water. By this time, Jay was ready to throw the tent out together with me, my brilliant ideas, and all of the camping gear. We all tried frantically to be useful and help him in every way by holding on to the poles despite the strong wind. I think Jay took pity on us seeing us so excited and trying so hard to help that he held on and continued trying to decipher how to put the tent up.

Fortunately, resourceful Jay is just the right type for this kind of predicament. He figured the tent situation out of logic and common sense and managed at last to put it up. By this time, we were soaked. It was pitch black, the mosquitoes had attacked us and had a feast with us. Annette was desperate to get to the bathroom. We were all hungry and tired, but we needed that ice because the meat was thawing out fast. There was just no time to be tired so we decided to leave Adele and our nephew with one lantern, a flashlight and a mountain of boxes to get some unpacking done while we went for the ice. After trying a number of stores, we finally found the precious commodity. Poor Adele and Pepi looked like two abandoned orphans in the dark campsite setting when we finally got back with ice. They had not been able to accomplish much because the contents of the boxes were not marked, and no one knew where to find anything. Only I who had done the packing had a vague idea of where the necessary items could be found. Exhausted, starved and still slapping mosquitoes, we finally were able to put things more or less in place and started a fire for grilling. In the darkness Jay dropped a steak on the sand. I broke a fruit jar. Even I the optimist was having second thoughts about whether this camping trip had been such a good idea after all. Maybe Jay had been right. If this was vacation and relaxation, I began to think it would have been better to have stayed home.

I was totally clueless as to the many problems that can come up to the inexperienced camper. I imagine this was the reason why my husband was so reluctant to the camping idea. He knew he had to face the adventure practically alone with just three girls and his 15-year old nephew to give him more moral support than practical support.

By midnight we were eating, and our sense of humor began to recover, so that we were able to laugh at ourselves and at all that had happened. It all appeared terribly funny after all. When we finally landed on our cots that night and closed our eyes to the beautiful starry night over us, I prayed and thanked God for having made the experience possible and for having helped us get there safely. Next morning, when we awoke to a gorgeous sunny morning, with the breeze filled with the smell of the sea and the sounds of nature all about us, I knew that it had all been worth doing, and that we were going to have a great time.

Things always look better during the day, but not so with our tent. It was quite a sloppy spectacle to behold, standing there with a lopsided distorted look as if it were ready to collapse any minute. We really ruined the neighborhood with all of the other good-looking well-set tents and campers around us. Laughing at our inexperience, we all helped Jay do a better job now that tension was behind us. From that moment on, everything improved, and we had a great time. In fact, we made many camping trips after, but none was as difficult or as funny as this first camping experience. This was first an idea, then a plan and the plan was executed. We faced the obstacles and adapted to the alternatives, and the idea became reality.

Our next dream: our sailboat. This had been Jay's big dream for many years. Because there were always so many other important dreams competing for attention and money, and there is a limit to what your finances can take, the sailboat dream had been temporarily put aside, but never forgotten or discarded. We both knew it would be some day, and its time came.

As we drove down to the Florida Keys watching the many beautiful sailboats on the water, Jay felt his dream very vividly, and we talked about it that day and in the days that followed. He was sure that sailing would be his favorite pastime and would replace golf. He knew as a family we would all enjoy it, especially now that we had son Stan, Adele's husband, who was like Jay, the outdoor type. It made a lot of sense, and I felt we really had waited long enough for this dream and had pushed it down the priority list too many times. Since Jay felt it was his dream more than ours, and he is an unselfish type, I knew he would not push for it unless I gave it impetus. I had now learned to find happiness by giving happiness, and even though

I am not the seafaring type, I plunged enthusiastically on the idea of getting the sailboat.

I assured Jay that he should have it, that life was much too short to forego dear dreams when they were attainable, and that the time was now. So, we figured our finances, just as we had done 27 years before to buy that maroon Chevy, and a month later, Jay had selected his sailboat within our price range but with all of the things he wanted. Before summer came, he was sailing all over Biscayne Bay in a 22-foot beautiful sailboat. Just as we thought, the whole family enjoyed the boat, and we had much fun with this new dream that became reality. However, that talk about sailing replacing golf was not quite true. Jay now sailed on weekends and played golf and tennis during week afternoons, but he was having one great time, and I loved it because he was happy, and a happy man makes a wonderful husband.

If you have done nothing more than dream up to now, you can change this pattern if you make the decision to plan, act in an organized way to achieve your goal and through prayer enlist the Lord as your Partner. You must discipline yourself to act out your plans step by step with perseverance and faith in God. You too will see most of your dreams come true. Maybe all!

RULE 5: ORGANIZE, PRAY, AND ACT OUT YOUR DREAMS.

CHAPTER 6

Give It All You Got

Enthusiasm and optimism are two key ingredients in a happy person's life. They furnish us with the fuel and energy to organize and act out our dreams. Through enthusiasm and optimism we add zest to life, and we have faith in today and tomorrow. They give us the impulse to give our dreams and plans all we've got.

Whether you are planning a backyard cookout or an African safari, each project, big or small, should be cause for fun and excitement . Life is short, and we must grasp every opportunity that can offer us happy moments. Your chances of cruising the Nile or escalating the Himalayas are a bit more remote than starting a vegetable garden, making a dress, or planning a small dinner party. So you might as well learn to get worked up about these smaller projects until the biggies come along so you will have that many more happy moments to enjoy. Everything is what you make of it, and it is in your hands to have a fun-filled interesting life or a dull boring one.

With me, enthusiasm and optimism are natural traits so I have not had to work at this attitude and principle as much as with other principles. I certainly did not learn optimism and enthusiasm from my mother who was a confirmed pessimist, so I am sure God gave me these natural assets out of his good heart to help me be a happier person. But, like everything else, enthusiasm can be cultivated. Do not allow yourself to be passive about anything good you may be planning or doing. Let yourself get excited. It is really so much fun when you let the spark of enthusiasm kindle.

Our friends told us that parties at our home were always fun. We both had developed a reputation within our social circle of being warm and good hosts. I believe the key reason for our success in this area was our enthusiasm. When I plan a dinner party, small or large, I make it a real project which I thoroughly enjoy and which gives me a source of stimulation. I plan all the details, do my hair, fix my nails, and get all dolled up as if I were expecting royalty. Even if it is just a small get together, I work with the same spunk as if it were a state dinner. I do not consider the task hard work but real fun.

Now in my older years I plan monthly family get-togethers so we can keep the family united and close. These get-togethers provide an opportunity to talk, relate, learn what is happening in everyone's lives and keeps us together as a family. Family is such an important treasure that we need to nurture and keep. These parties give us the chance also to see our great grandchildren in action, enjoy watching their progress and development and soak in their demonstrations of affection. I give our family parties the same enthusiasm and preparation that I did my parties years ago. When it is all over, and all have left, I sit and look back at the entire evening with tremendous joy and satisfaction. I know similar get-togethers can happen in most homes and can be planned with the same enthusiasm as mine if you set your heart to it. Try it. You will see what a difference it makes to get involved in a project actively instead of passively.

Enthusiasm can be applied to every plan and to everything we do. After all, when you come right down to it, what is living if you strip off the gusto you can get from every good thing you may have the chance to do? Do not knock anything that may come your way. You can be turned on by almost every pleasant thing if you set your mind to it. I have always been the type to get worked up with all my projects which most of the time are small. Friends and people close to me tell me they find this trait stimulating even to them. Years ago, it may have been a beach picnic, vacation plans or sailing. Now it could be Christmas, or some small remodeling project at home, or buying something inexpensive but new to perk up the wardrobe for the new season, or planning a family birthday. Whatever the project, I have always made it a source of happiness and injected excitement into it.

Closely linked with enthusiasm is another important attitude which can make you see life quite differently—rosier and happier. Optimism in your life is like putting on a pair of rosy sunglasses. Everything is how you look at it. Perhaps, this can best be exemplified by the old story we have all heard of the optimist and the pessimist looking at the same half-filled glass of water, and each seeing it differently only because of their difference in attitude. Truly, to the optimist the glass was almost full while the pessimist actually saw it practically empty. Yet both were looking at the same identical glass with the same amount of water. Similarly, an optimistic or pessimistic attitude can make us see our lives as great or not so great. Right and positive attitudes are extremely important to our happiness. They contribute to good general physical and mental health.

A positive and realistically optimistic attitude is healthy and can make us capable of coping with life as it is. The pessimist, on the other hand, is always seeing disaster and doom in everything. More than half of the pessimist's life is spent brooding about all the bad things they are certain will occur. Pessimism breeds negative attitudes and needless fear which in turn affects your health. Pessimists do little to improve their lot as they have accepted their fate. They kill such a beautiful thing as hope that keeps the optimist fighting and alive.

There have been days when I have been tired because of too much activity and not enough sleep, and everything has appeared bleak and grey. Every small problem was like a major crisis. I have felt listless and apathetic. The traffic light just would never change, and all of the small things which I usually enjoy would do nothing for me on those days that my attitude was not bright and positive. Yet those very same every-day problems can face me when my attitude is positive and optimistic, and they appear quite different.

Fortunately for me, when I have one of these days, I can recognize that basically I am still a happy person and that my temporary poor attitude is the real culprit and cause for feeling low and defeated. I am aware that tomorrow when I am rested, my attitude will again revert to my normal positive optimistic outlook. But, those bad days also give me the opportunity to see that everything is the way you perceive it. Nothing had changed in my life during the low period. Nothing was really brighter or gloomier—-it was just me. The following day, when I am back to my usual optimistic self, and everything looks brighter and problems appear minimal, nothing is really better or rosier, it is just me and my improved attitude.

For years I worked under an aura of doom as PanAm faced severe financial problems. From day to day, our economic status dwindled and insecurity reigned. The person with whom I worked and I knew the situation was not good, but we also knew life had to go on. We believed things would probably improve rather than deteriorate. We continued to travel, change cars, and carry on with our lives, always thinking positive. Some of our pessimistic co-workers literally stopped living, preparing for the worse. They dared not do anything that required financial output. Doomsday did arrive, but 11 years later. We lived happily and productively those 11 years! We survived the blow, and still had the good times and experiences to show for those years while our pessimistic friends stopped living, merely existed, waiting for the fatal day.

I choose to be the realistic optimist because I want to believe that the best will happen, but I also want to feel propelled to do something to make the best happen. Optimism that is not coupled with action and a realistic evaluation of the situation can lead to idle wishful thinking which will stop the person from taking positive action to make good things happen. We should always plan on the assumption that the best will happen, but be prepared to accept the second best, just in case, and then learn to recognize the hidden virtues the second best can offer. Sometimes, the second best may turn out to be best after all. There is much truth in the saying "all things always happen for the best." I always hope for the best, believe it will be, and strive in every way to bring it about. However, when sometimes the best I had wished does not materialize, I accept the alternate or second best as the best I was unable to recognize before. It usually turns out that way, and if nothing else, accepting a reversal to my dream in the right spirit, already sets me in a good frame of mind for happy living.

Live with zest and give it all you got!

RULE 6: BE ENTHUSIASTIC AND HAVE AN OPTIMISTIC AND POSTIVE OUTLOOK ON LIFE.

CHAPTER 7

Who's Perfect? Stay With It!

Perfection just does not exist. When you become perfection worshippers, usually you not only feel eternally unsuccessful but accomplish little because you are paralyzed by your inability to attain the degree of perfection you seek. When perfectionists are not successful in reaching the perfection they so desire, they feel disappointed and disillusioned. Worse yet, they will frequently never start any project or give it up along the way because it could not be accomplished with the degree of perfection they demanded, and discouragement sets in.

Perfectionists appear to be experts on whatever subject they have at hand, checking all minute details closely before starting a project. Often, they never go beyond their knowledge-gathering efforts becoming overwhelmed with its magnitude. They then justify their lack of accomplishment by reasoning that it was caused by their demand for more and their inability to be satisfied with anything less than perfect. Consequently, many times they seem to remain unfulfilled with their frustrated dreams.

Perfection is required and should be sought to the maximum degree humanly possible only when dealing with highly complex matters and activities in which precision is mandatory or when safety plays an important part. In those special cases, there is no room for imperfection. Other than such demanding activities or projects, most other endeavors should be approached with persistency and tenacity striving for excellence but not consumed by a drive for perfection. Frequently an unrealistic quest for perfection is motivated by personal pride. You should steer away from the perfection trap that prevents you from realizing results.

Non perfectionists may make imperfect headway, but with each less than perfect accomplishment, they get closer to their goal. The person who does not demand perfection but persists will make steady and gradual gains to the amazement of the perfectionist who cannot believe that someone so undemanding can achieve success. They fail to understand that it is better to relentlessly stick to a project, perform to the best of your capabilities and capture the sweet reward of some achievement even when the results are not perfect. The non perfectionist realizes that this imperfect achievement is far better than being immobilized by a thirst for perfection. People that persist without considering perfection as the only goal usually end up getting more done. In fact, many times they achieve as much perfection as is humanly possible. More importantly, by not seeking perfection they very often savor the taste of fulfillment in their projects and ventures because they did not allow inertia to creep up on them seeking perfection. In contrast, many times perfectionists get lost by the wayside demanding too much of themselves and others.

Another vital aspect to be considered is the time and efforts utilized in seeking perfection. On those instances in which perfectionists do not become discouraged, they usually have spent a disproportionate and unjustifiable amount of time and energy in their project.

Many times perfectionists end up with the same results or even less satisfactory results than that obtained by non-perfectionists. I am not certain, but I attribute the results of this absurd compulsion as God's way of mocking perfectionists for their useless efforts primarily spurred by pride.

When we moved to Miami, we wanted to buy a home right away rather than rent. We also wanted a home that would be comparable in comfort to the one we left behind in Cuba so we would not feel depressed with the change we had been forced to make. During our first weekend in Miami, we fell in love with a model home in a new housing development and decided instantly to buy the same home which would be custom built for us. It appeared to have everything we were seeking: the layout was functional for our family's needs, the price was right, it had possibilities for future growth and expansion, it was close to a school for our 6-year old, and the neighborhood was nice. We felt we would be happy there. What more could we want?

A few weeks later when I began working at PanAm, a co-worker who was a perfectionist in the true sense of the word, with not one hair out of place and not one wrinkle in her attire, told me of her house-hunting efforts, a project to which she had dedicated years. She boasted of how carefully she had checked many houses with her demand for perfection before making a choice of that caliber. Hearing her story, I admit I was somewhat embarrassed over the little knowledge we had shown in the area of house buying by her standards. She had been living in Miami for years; we had just arrived and had already bought a house. How uninformed and unprepared I felt. Her apparent knowledge of house selecting as compared to ours was striking. Our abnormally fast decision to buy a house based on just basics and instinct began to concern me. I began to seriously doubt whether our quick decision had been correct and to question our settling for practically the first house we liked.

All my feelings of inadequacy vanished when one morning she arrived at the office announcing she had at last found the perfect house of her dreams that fulfilled her every expectation. I couldn't wait to see the literature she had brought. To my total surprise and complete satisfaction, it was the exact identical house as ours built by the same builder, but in another area of town. I had to hold myself not to burst into laughter. Internally, I was beaming with pride. This major decision had taken us only days; she, the perfectionist, had spent years to come up with the same house.

Next, she fussed and debated over the type of grass she wanted, had her husband pull out the grass provided by the builders and planted a very special and expensive type of grass which supposedly would be more resistant to lawn plagues. Once more, she knew so much about this subject. We accepted the ordinary grass that came with the house rather than get involved with the additional expense and work. We watered and cared for our mediocre grass, and to date, 55 years later; we still have the same original ordinary grass which I admit is far from perfect, interwoven with weeds here and there, but our lawn looks very presentable at minimal cost. My friend's superior grass became infected in a short time, and she had to start over again from scratch. We worked and spent much less than my perfectionist co-worker, and yet still obtained better and very acceptable results. To have wasted such important time and efforts to satisfy her perfectionist pride appeared totally ridiculous to me. Almost laughable!

My brother/cousin Joe was an average student and a typical boy who was much more interested in play than books. His mother never lost heart. She persistently encouraged him with much love to study and not to give up. She always stressed the importance of keeping at it and of doing his best, whatever that might be. His father was a doctor, and they had high hopes for him to become a doctor also. I do not think Joe was very motivated at first in this direction, but because of his good nature and the faith his parents had in him, he did not want to let them down. He entered Pre-Medical School at the University of Florida, and his first four years of college were far from perfect. In fact, anyone with a perfectionist mind would not have continued. Instead, he persisted, spurred on by his parents' encouragement, and did not give up. Then, as he matured, in his last four years during which he had to confront many setbacks which would have easily discouraged anyone, he became motivated of himself and plunged into his studies with enthusiasm. This motivation stemmed from his own desire to achieve, not that of his parents, and he made it. Had he been a perfectionist, he probably would have desisted along the way when his grades were less than desirable, but instead he held on and with each small imperfect victory, he gained strength and enthusiasm to do more, and in his last years his grades were excellent.

All of us know young people who have become discouraged immediately when studies became tough, or they could not study under perfect circumstances. They just gave up. Many of these young people are frequently more brilliant than the persistent student who stays with it. Intelligence alone does not make the goal. It takes dedication and tenacity more than brilliance to make steady and gradual headway, imperfect as your achievements may be, to reach the goal line without losing heart.

I was a good student and book learning has always been easy for me, but practical manual abilities I do not possess. It is much harder for me to do things that involve my hands than to figure a trigonometry problem. If I had been a perfectionist, I would never have learned to type or drive a stick shift car. I would have shunned away from cooking with its cutting and carving requirements because I could not accomplish these skills with any degree of perfection. I did well doing things that involved only the intellect but failed miserably with my clumsy hands. However, I mastered typing by keeping at it, and although I don't consider myself the fastest typist in the world, I am above average. By persistency, I have also managed well with my cutting abilities although these abilities do not come natural to me, and I do detest them. Regardless of how proficiently or not I can perform these culinary functions, I am totally capable of producing a tasty meal which is the end result. I am quite content with my accomplishments in this area even though they are far from perfect. Through perseverance I gained enough dexterity in the areas that were not natural for me. Had I demanded perfection from myself, I probably would not have attempted to overcome my inadequacies to whatever extent I have. This accomplishment has provided me with a sense of satisfaction that has made me happy with myself.

If you recognize yourself as a perfectionist, lacking in persistency, start to work on a plan without delay and stick to the job even when you cannot see results. Decide what it is that you want, work for it passionately and when it happens, settle for that which mostly resembles your dream if your exact dream is not realistically possible. Do not lose time waiting for the perfect situation which might never happen. Remember that while you are doing nothing, immobilized with all the knowledge you have gathered, others, less demanding, are already enjoying the same thing you could have. Perhaps, what you achieve is not as perfect as your unrealistic dream, but still much better by comparison than what you now have or will have because of your perfectionist inertia.

RULE 7: DO NOT DEMAND PERFECTION OF YOURSELF OR OTHERS. INSTEAD, STAY WITH IT AND BE PERSISTENT.

CHAPTER 8

Keep Busy

Happy people are busy people and busy people are happy people. Activity and feeling good go hand in hand. Each day of our lives should be filled with plans and activity. We all know there will always be some things to be done that are not particularly what we enjoy, but if you recognize they are necessary and inescapable, you should do them quickly and get them out of the way so you can move on to better and more enjoyable activities.

Finding a way to make unpleasant chores more palatable is important, and believe me, it can be done. Sometimes, simply thinking of the rewarding results our efforts will bring can do the trick. This is true when you think of enjoying a clean fresh home after it has been cleaned or visualizing a pretty yard after having worked hard on it. Sometimes, merely feeling the sense of having completed an unpleasant task can push you to get it done quickly. You can also lighten the task by adding a pleasant ingredient such as music or a tasty refreshment or snack.

For many years before I could afford outside help, I did my house cleaning on weekends or Friday nights if I was not too tired. I dislike cleaning because I find so many more interesting things in

Keep Busy

which to spend time and efforts that I cannot help but feel that these strictly routine repetitive chores interfere with my free time. But, I also realize that I like to live in a clean and attractive home, and I get much pleasure out of seeing the house in order and clean. I beam when my husband compliments our home or years ago when my daughter Annette would tell me she was proud of our home when she had friends over. These feelings give me the impulse for attacking the job as quickly as possible without further procrastination. With a selection of my favorite records before too long I gradually begin to overcome my initial inertia and become more enthusiastic about the work. As I finish each area, I gain stamina to tackle the next because the end appears closer, and I can already sense the good feeling that my house is clean, uncluttered, and organized. Undoubtedly, music helps alleviate the burden for me.

When I got it all done Friday night, even though I may have pushed hard and had gone to bed late and tired, all my efforts were compensated when I woke up late Saturday morning to a clean and fresh house with the unpleasant job behind me. I felt like a queen. It was great to know that Saturday and Sunday were mine to do the things I wanted and enjoyed. This was my way of licking an unpleasant but necessary chore.

Before getting involved with something you do not enjoy, you should first be certain the unpleasant job is really necessary or required of you as part of a commitment. If not, then you should definitely strike it out entirely from your day because life is much too important and brief to be wasted on unpleasant activities that are not required. Why should you polish silver that is just going to be stored away and will need to be polished again when needed? You should not suffer ironing your wash and wear garments when they look great only because your mother taught you that clothes should be ironed. You certainly do not need to vacuum every day, nor wash every day, nor wash your windows every month. Take a close look at the things you are doing that you do not enjoy and streamline the unpleasant duties so that you don't give these more time and effort than absolutely necessary. Once you are convinced the disliked work must be done, and no approach seems to work to help you get started, just stop putting it off one second more and plunge to it and get it out of your life quickly so it will haunt you no further. What a great feeling to know that now you are free for more pleasant and enjoyable activities.

Leisure time is also very important, and you must learn to enjoy your leisure time without feelings of guilt. Keeping busy is not limited only to performing required tasks or fulfilling commitments but it includes also doing those things you enjoy. Leisure is not to be confused with inactivity because we all need to pause here and there for a break. There are many ways of keeping busy leisurely as reading, writing, painting, sewing and indulging in any pastime or hobby which can be done without stress and with no deadline to meet. The idea is to keep entertained and happy with projects, hobbies, sports, and whatever activity you may enjoy. Even just sitting and planning can keep you happily busy. It is great fun to enjoy moments of disconnect and to engage in activities just for sheer enjoyment.

However, drifting meaningless through the day without a purpose, bored, feeling tired without having done much, having no interest or desire to tackle anything, are all signs there is something very wrong with you, physically or mentally, and you need to address the problem. However, if that is not the case, you need to get on your feet and fight the lethargy with planned activity. This is one instance when it would be better to exaggerate and overdo to break the undesirable pattern. You can later pull back and bring your activities to a more normal level, but at first, fight the bed and couch habit with intense activity.

When I advocate keeping busy, I am not condemning rest. We are not machines, and there is a limit to the amount of activity an individual can handle. You must be able to relax and rest, but the kind of rest that feels good because you have earned it by being active and productive. If you stay in bed all day or just sit around most of the day, day in and day out, this kind of rest is not natural and can only make you feel bored and unhappy. This type of inactivity can only be justified when a person is sick or has been overworked over a period of time. Rest is necessary when excessive activity has taxed you, but any other idle moments will merely produce monotony and apathy.

One of the happiest persons I have ever known was my father. He was a simple and good man that everyone loved. He was happy with everything in his life. Although I know there were many things that made Dad such a content man, I am certain that his continuous activity contributed very much to his happiness. He enjoyed excellent health until approximately age 90 because he kept as active and busy as in his younger years. I do not remember my Dad without a project. He did not play golf or fish. His hobby was working and puttering around the house, but each project he planned and almost immediately put into action, brought him a tremendous source of satisfaction. Although he worked hard and untiring at his projects, he also had the ability to enjoy well deserved leisure and relaxation. Many times I saw him feeling exhausted, stop to shower, and with his ever beloved cigar, succumb gratefully into the couch, with feet stretched on the coffee table, to enjoy a well-earned afternoon or evening of television. But, the next day, he would again surrender himself to the project with the same furor and intent of the previous day. My Dad built doghouses, patios, tool sheds, workbenches, and awnings. He installed sprinkler systems, paneled, painted, cemented, put up fences, tiled floors and walls, and did just about every job that could come up in a house. There was no end to his energy and desire to be useful. He never had to do these things strictly as a responsibility required of him. He simply derived enjoyment from accomplishing his projects, knew how to use his time effectively and completed each project he embraced.

This anecdote of my father will always remain for the family as a humorous remembrance of the man who always wanted to do something productive with his time. Once, all dressed up, with bags packed, just waiting with the rest of the family to leave for the airport to catch a plane for a three-week European vacation, we could not find him anywhere in the house. Time was running short to get to the airport, but he was nowhere to be found. Finally, he appeared outside caulking some crevices around a window which he thought could be vulnerable while we were away. Wiping his dusty hands with the clean nice handkerchief my mother had carefully provided for the trip, he was happily ready for his European trip. His reasoning was that if he had ten free minutes, and he was not tired, why just sit idly around waiting when he could take advantage of this time to do something useful. This is typical of happy busy people. Every minute is put to good use, not necessarily because it is required of them but because happy people like to be active.

When you habitually waste precious time doing nothing you will be frustrated with yourself. To realize at the end of a day that you have not accomplished anything productive or yet worse, to know that you did not even attempt to do so, can leave you with a sense of worthlessness.

You can do a great deal more than you think if you organize yourself with a list of things to do, including both those you should do and those you enjoy doing. A list will help you use your time effectively each day so that you do first the more important and necessary things. As you scratch off from the list, you will feel so efficient and happy with yourself. Without a list, you might just think about the many things you have to do or would like to do, but with no plan of action, you will never get beyond the thinking stage.

I am a list fiend and have been ever since I was a teenager. I find I get a great more done because of my lists. For instance, if you have a list of things to do while you are out during your lunch hour, you could probably do a number of them within the same area, if you are aware of them. There may be a card shop, a discount store, and a gift shop all in the same shopping area. My list tells me I need a wedding card, shampoo, blades for my husband, and a birthday gift so I can solve all of these items in one stop. If I did not have a list, chances are I might stop to get the item foremost in my mind but I might not remember the wedding card because I would not need it until a week's time. The shampoo might slip my mind until I find myself in the shower, and I would forget about my husband's blades until he reminds me again he's down to his last one. This would mean I would have to exert duplicate energy and time by stopping another day for these items which I could have accomplished all in one shot.

A list also helps you get organized by allowing you to see all your requirements at a glance. This lets you prioritize so you can accomplish each day during the week a number of the more important and pressing things without doing more than you can handle, but without loss of time. If you do not have a list, you might do very little or anything at all on Monday and Tuesday because the whole week is ahead, and you really are not aware of all you have to do. Then, on Wednesday night it dawns on you that you just have two working days left before the week is over to accomplish all that you needed to do. Chaos takes over as you frantically scramble trying to catch up without a plan only because you never took the time to put it on paper. Some of the important items will not be done or are done poorly under pressure. This need not happen if you get organized. You probably devoted time earlier in the week to lesser important things simply because you had no idea that you had so much to do. You will blame your predicament to lack of time when actually if you had prepared a list, had checked it, and organized your time according to priorities, you really did have time to get a great deal more done than what you accomplished.

My master list is endless as I continue adding to it because I am alive, and my mind is constantly producing new ideas and plans. Realistically, I acknowledge that all of the items on my master list are not important and that I will probably never be able to do them all. This I accept and I am not frustrated about, but I still keep these things on my master list just in case optimistically I ever find the time. The master list will not allow an item to slip my mind, and maybe, just maybe, I might be able to do a few someday. I will extract from my master list the important items that I need to tackle each week and work on them each day, doing the most urgent first so that what is important will get done. If I have five free minutes during my day which can be put to good use, there will always be some item on my list that can be handled during that short time. I can water a plant that's crying out for moisture or I can make a quick call which could be handled with a minute or two. If I did not have a list to remind me, those few minutes would be lost because it would seem too short a time to think of something to do or to get involved with a major project. Later, absorbed with a more complex project, chances are that the plant will go without water or the call will not be made. The list guides you so you can determine what you can handle at any given free time according to its complexity and time-consuming nature. I have been living this way for years, and it works.

Life is for living and doing. Please do not just lie around in your robe or your pajamas over that coffee cup longer than necessary. Please do not get back into bed after you have had a good night's rest. Get up and go. There is a bright and good day ahead awaiting you with at least sixteen useful hours and a wonderful world with millions of interesting things to do. Go out and meet it head on! You will be happy you did.

RULE 8: KEEP BUSY, EARN YOUR REST, MAKE A "TO DO" LIST, DON'T PROCASTINATE AND JUST GET THE JOB DONE.

CHAPTER 9

Two Magical Words: "I'm Sorry"

Two small words that can mean so much to others and do so much for us: "I'm sorry." False pride or stubbornness can bring us much misery. On occasions, we are all going to make mistakes, and we are going to be at fault in some way. As only imperfect human beings, struggling to improve ourselves, why should it be so difficult to apologize and to admit you were wrong? Put your pride on a shelf — — you do not need it if it is going to interfere with your happiness, and it will, if it stops you from saying "I'm sorry" to someone who deserves it. Everything can change when you are able to utter those two magical words.

It is really so simple that it is surprising to see how much difficulty you can create for yourself by not being able to admit you have made a mistake and to offer your regrets. You enjoy receiving this admission from others — -why is it so hard when it is your turn to admit an error? I have little or no pride when it comes to apologizing. I will apologize to anyone without the least difficulty if I have been wrong or at fault in any way. I have found without exception that people react very nicely to apologies. In fact, sometimes they are so unaccustomed to receiving apologies, and they themselves may have difficulty apologizing that they seem to be taken aback by a frank spontaneous admission of mistake from another person. The unexpected apology causes reaction in them that cannot be but favorable.

Apologies should not be restricted for certain people only. We should make a habit of apologizing to anyone who deserves an apology. For instance, I have apologized many times to my children when I have realized I have been wrong, and I have found my children have appreciated this from me. When you have overcome this pride problem and apologizing comes easy to you, you will see how much simpler life can be and how much your action can add to your happiness and that of others. In a way, it all goes back to being happy by making others happy. The person who can say "I'm sorry"' feels relieved while at the same time making another person feel better too just with words that convey an admission of error. Do not let yourself be caught in an ego trap that can only bring you inner conflicts and unhappiness when it is so easy and so beautiful to say "I'm sorry" when you have erred.

This is particularly true and important in man/woman relationships. Even at times when you feel certain you were not at fault, if your partner cannot bring himself or herself to apologize, for heaven's sake, don't prolong the agony and lose precious living time because your pride gets in the way. Between two people who are truly in love and their love has been amply demonstrated and proven by their actions on numerous occasions, the matter of who apologizes is unimportant. If you happen to be the one with greater humility, less ego and greater intelligence that allows you to recognize the unimportance of the problem, by all means, you should put an end to the situation by apologizing. Although you may be convinced you are due the apology yourself, you will be surprised to see the results. In all probability, your partner may deep down know he or she is at fault, but just has an ego issue that does not allow saying "I'm sorry" easily. However, when hit by your wiser attitude, he or she will feel embarrassed and an apology may come after all. In any case, besides being a teaching moment, you will have put an end to the unpleasant situation and stopped the foolish loss of time.

I have practiced this myself with my husband. It is much harder for him to say "I'm sorry" than it is for me. This I know. I guess as a boy he grew up with the idea that apologizing could be taken as a sign of weakness for a man, or maybe it is just that his pride makeup is tougher to crack than mine. Since I have no doubt that he loves me, I have never allowed this to come between us. On occasion I have fished and waited for an apology when I have felt certain that he was wrong. When this has not worked, I have tried to discuss the problem with him so he could see what was obvious to me, if analyzed objectively. Sometimes this has worked, but there have been times, for some inexplicable reason, that nothing has produced an apology from him. Then, rather than waste time waiting for the apology and getting upset because of the lack of it, I have taken another approach. I have told him that I understood that maybe he was right, and I just had not seen things his way. I made him understand that regardless of who was right or wrong, we should forget the whole incident because I knew he loved me and I loved him, and there was no point in wasting any more time on the matter. This approach was enough to make him melt, smile, give me a kiss and tell me he was sorry also because he realized he had also provoked the problem in some way. Both of us were saved unhappiness because we put our pride aside.

This strategy works more between husband and wife and people in love, but sometimes it can be effective even with others. I have found many times that when I start in an apologetic fashion with someone, it becomes much easier for that person to also apologize. I have had many examples in my life with people I have worked for and with, with friends, and just with people in general, that prove that saying "I'm sorry" can work wonders. Because I have practiced this principle in so many ways with such good results, and I have experienced such a great feeling each time I have pronounced the two magical words when I have been at fault, I really encourage everyone to make this principle a part of your way of living.

Apologizing when an apology is due is a sure and simple way of adding happiness to your life.

RULE #9: LEARN TO SAY "I'M SORRY."

CHAPTER 10

Callous Your Feelings

O verly sensitive people are not very popular. People do not want to be bothered with persons whose feelings are so raw and vulnerable that they have to be pampered constantly and treated with extreme care. That's no fun. Callous your feelings and equip yourself with a good sense of humor so you can endure reasonable wear and tear.

First of all, you must eliminate those horrible feelings that make you think that people are constantly doing things just to hurt you or with ulterior motives. Such susceptibility in most cases does not have sound basis and exists only in your mind. Most people are not trying to hurt you, and it does not take long to determine if someone is really trying to offend you. You can then decide your course of action in these isolated cases. But, in the meantime, fight the feeling with all your might because people do not like to have to be so careful and special in associating with others. Super-sensitive people make us feel uncomfortable, and usually have few friends because it becomes too burdensome to deal with them. Strengthen that sense of humor and your sense of self-worth.

I have had to work more at this principle. When I was growing up, I was inclined to be very sensitive, and my feelings were easily bruised. I felt everyone owed me special care in dealing with me. Since I myself tried hard not to hurt other people's feelings, I reasoned that everyone should be as careful. But, when I realized my sensitivity was causing me much misery and certainly not making me very popular, I began to fight the feeling of inadequacy and fear that accompanies super-sensitivity. At first, as in all cases of changing behavior patterns, it was difficult, and I only faked not being hurt, when I really was. I laughed off things, even though the tears were inside, but at least, I had taken the first step, and people were not aware that I was hurt. I faked I could handle situations I really could not, but in the process the positive effects that resulted from faking convinced me gradually that I had no true basis for feeling hurt. I realized that whatever had provoked the feeling was not targeted to hurt me personally.

Today, I feel I have overcome the problem and need not fake anymore. I have learned to callous my feelings to my advantage and the pleasure of others who do not have to be bothered with my petty sensitivity. I find my friends appreciate this quality in me because they know I never take things personally nor require much pampering. They know that if they do not call, I will call them. They need not worry if they forget my birthday because I am convinced it had nothing to do with caring. It is great to be rid of those terrible sensitive feelings that can needlessly take away so much from happiness.

Most of the time sensitive people suffer for unjustified reasons. They visualize what does not exist and magnify things out of proportion. What was forgetfulness is interpreted as being shunned. As a result, they react in such a way, they actually create animosity for themselves when the supposedly offending party, totally unaware of what is going on, cannot understand the sensitive person's reactions. After working at it, I now can analyze in a cool manner situations that would have hurt me before. I simply ask myself whether the supposedly offending person has any reason to act wrongly against me. I also analyze whether this person's past actions have given me ample positive evidence to believe there was no offense intended. If I conclude there is no cause for that person to shun me or to act incorrectly with me, and our prior interactions reinforce this, I justify the questionable action and do not allow it to bother me. If I cannot reach such a clear cut conclusion, I have learned to forget the incident and let time tell. It usually turns out there was nothing wrong or malicious behind the action, and I saved myself some worry and upset.

I have frequently found that feelings can be very touchy with people who are part of a minority group in a community. Inevitably, minority groups are discriminated against to some extent when they become large and affect the rest of the community in a significant way. In essence, even though they are still a minority, they are large enough that they cannot be overlooked. This is not the case when the minority group is small and as a group is practically unnoticed. On the contrary, when there are just a few persons in a community belonging to a minority, many times they take on greater importance and are treated as special people. It is only when the minority becomes large enough to affect many aspects of an area that discrimination sets in. Add to this the fact that there will always be people who find it difficult to accept others who are different from them and will not accept them under any condition. These are people who can only see the negative aspects and never appreciate anything else in those who are different from them.

Callous Your Feelings

Between the two factors, discrimination will arise. As a result, many people belonging to large minorities are prone to carry chips on their shoulders and develop minority sensitivity. Certain they are rejected by everyone outside their group, they either react with feelings of inferiority or sometimes with an arrogant air of superiority. Either way they add to the already existing problem by making themselves the target of further dislike from the bigots who then feel more justified in their discrimination. The problem compounds when the minority persons fail to project a true image of themselves to people who have no prejudice and are fair minded. The solution to this problem is for persons belonging to a minority to show themselves not as inferior or superior, but as the regular people they truly are who are similar to those who find them different. If they do not, they create for themselves further unpopularity even among those who are not bigots.

I have been part of a minority group all my life, and I can honestly say I have never felt sensitive about this although at times the thought has been placed in my mind by others more sensitive than I. I have never thought I would be rejected just because I had a Spanish name or looked Hispanic. In my mind, I always believed that even if some narrow-minded person did see me different, that would be the exception. I was certain that most people would accept me for me if I did not isolate myself but mixed into the community. I have experienced this to be true.

I was born and grew up in Tampa where there was a large Latino community made up of first and second generation immigrants from Spain, Cuba, and Sicily. So much so, there is a section of town called Ybor City that was so totally Latin you practically did not need English to survive in my time. I went to school with children whose names were Fernandez, Lopez, Gonzalez or Spoto, Cacciatore, Ficarrota and the like. I knew very few Smiths or Jones when I was growing up.

In looking back I believe the reason why I managed not to develop minority sensitivity and escaped becoming a misfit falling in the crack in the middle was because my parents never put the thought in my mind. I also had the advantage of visiting Cuba every summer to visit with my mother's family. This gave me the opportunity of actually seeing how it was on the other side where Cubans were not a minority but regular people and not target of discrimination. I realized that people there were like those at home. There were good and bad people, there were lower class people, middle class and upper class people, there were well-educated and uneducated people, clean and dirty people, decent and indecent people. There were all kinds just like everywhere else. There in Cuba where they were not a minority they did not have a chip on their shoulders because they belonged. I think this awareness that my background was neither better nor worse than that of anyone else helped me develop a healthy sense of self-esteem as well as pride in my roots. This self-esteem did not allow me to fear I would not be accepted.

Over and over again I have seen that most people are good and do not discriminate on an individual basis. We all crack jokes about ethnic groups: Puerto Ricans, Mexicans, Jews, and we all know the many Polish jokes that go around, but most of us accept or reject people on an individual basis. When I finished Junior High, my dream was to attend Hillsborough High School which was considered the best in town at the time with a terrific football team that were State champions. It had been the high school my cousins had attended. Hillsborough High was quite distant from Ybor City at the time, and few Latinos attended that school, but went instead to a school closer to Ybor that had a majority Latino student body. My Junior High friends cautioned me not to go to Hillsborough because I would not be given a chance to participate in anything. I never even considered the warning. In fact, it bothered me to even think this could be true. I was so sure I would not have any problems. The challenge for me was to prove that if you can make yourself worthy of acceptance, you are accepted by most.

I was very happy to be chosen by my homeroom during my first semester to represent them in the Student Council. My Latino friends could not believe it. In my junior year I was elected to the National Honor Society which tested both faculty and students since both voted. It was tough competition as only a few were chosen from an extensive list of students with high averages. I can still remember vividly when the names began to be called that my heart skipped a beat or two. I was torn with confidence and lack of it. I wanted so much to be elected. When my name was called I barely understood it because it was a difficult name to pronounce for English-speaking persons, and I nearly died as I went up the stage. At that moment I knew that I was just another student who had been recognized for me. This was one of the greatest moments in my teen life, and above all, it proved to me that what I had believed was true: people do not discriminate on a one-on-one basis if you make yourself worthy of their respect. You have to work harder at it perhaps, but in the end, you will be accepted by normal people who just see the true you.

So if you too happen to belong to a minority group, please don't carry that chip and think everyone is against you. Instead, mix, come forward, prove your worth, and you will overcome the feeling of sensitivity that makes you think you are different. It is true that members of large minorities perhaps have to try a little more sometimes to prove their worth for those who cannot easily accept people who are not like them, but this should be taken as a challenge without bitterness. Please, do not run off by yourself with your own kind, do not feel inferior or superior, be your very best in every way, callous your feelings for the bigots who might be around, and move up to that immense majority who is ready to accept you once they realize you really are just like them. Only you can tell them this.

My two daughters grew up in Miami where a similar parallel situation to Tampa in the 1920s-1940s developed with the large influx of Cuban exiles as well as other ethnic groups into South Florida. Yet neither has ever felt discrimination. In fact, my oldest girl merged so into the so-called "WASP" community that my little dark-haired Rodriguez was one of the most popular girls throughout her school years. She was a Student Council member, Homecoming Princess, and a Flagette in an almost totally non-Hispanic school. She mixed with everyone, and I do not think she has ever considered herself different. She dated non-Hispanic boys and married a very "WASP" young man whom we love very much. I have never heard my youngest, Annette, speak of feeling discriminated. I do not believe she was ever aware of being a target of discrimination even though when it was her turn to grow up, the Hispanic community was much larger than in Adele's time and therefore more susceptible of being a force to be discriminated against. She always went forward, mixed, considered herself like everyone else, and never knew anything else.

Because of all of the above, I know you can overcome if you feel different or are just simply abnormally sensitive. One of the first steps is to callous your feelings. Whether you belong to a minority or not, there is no place for sensitivity in relating with people. Remove this handicap and free yourself of many hours of misery. I did it, and so can you.

RULE #10: DO NOT BE SUPERSENSITIVE. CALLOUS THOSE FEELINGS AND BOOST YOUR SELF ESTEEM.

CHAPTER 11

Keep Your Cool

There is no room in life for pettiness. Life is much too short and time much too valuable to be so wasted. Vital energy and time should not be spent in petty arguments and disputes which upset us and serve no other purpose than perhaps to prove some meaningless point. Save all your steam for justifiable situations, and on occasions there are some. Anger is a perfectly normal human reaction that at times cannot be avoided totally, but when you let this emotion take over your lives and become your master, then you are in trouble. You cannot permit this condition to become a way of life, becoming annoyed and irritated over every small incident that occurs in your daily lives.

Through the years I have learned not to argue over anything petty, unimportant or controversial. I do not care if I am judged as a conformist or a hypocrite because of this philosophy. I know no one can make me accept what I do not believe, even if I do not dispute it, and getting into a petty argument over it will probably not change the other person's position either. So what is there to be gained by arguing? Some people seem to enjoy these insignificant and controversial discussions which solve nothing or achieve anything but to get themselves and others in a bad mood. I refuse to allow these people to get me involved in their morbid way of passing time and will not play their foolish game. If I know I arrived at a certain time, but some such person insists it was five or ten minutes later, I will not argue the point unless those minutes mean my losing something very important, but I will not argue just to prove I was right. Either I will accept I was wrong, which could easily be, or if I am convinced I was right, I will merely state my position but qualify it in a way that would give the person contesting the issue the chance to save face. No one will get me to waste time on an unimportant argument. It just isn't worth it to me. It is amazing to see how people can get uptight over such foolish insignificant matters as "Who put this here?" or "Who left the door open?' and the like.

In most cases people recognize firmness and strength when expressed calmly and respectfully. Whenever this is not the case, then it is the right time to perhaps get a little tougher, if need be, but not until you have tried the cool road first and are convinced it did not produce results. You will find you can save yourself much unnecessary anger which cannot but ruin some precious moments of your life. Losing your cool affects your health, certainly does not make you well liked, makes you act irrationally and foolishly, and can cause you embarrassment later when you simmer down. I believe these are sufficient reasons to attempt to curtail this destructive emotion.

I have numerous examples of the many negative results that come from losing your temper. Each incident has remained with me and belittled the angry person in my view in such a way that I actually felt embarrassed for their reactions.

In one such altercation, an office associate with a fiery temper pounced on me unfairly about a problem over which I had no control.

This man, who lived perennially angry and bothered, acting and reacting all eight hours of his working day, would not take control of himself long enough to listen to my explanations to understand what had happened. He could only reason that things had not been done in the manner he required, causing him inconvenience, and this made him very but very upset. He was livid, his face white with anger, and he acted like a mad man. I know if I would have had a similar temper, lady or no lady, we would have had a fist fight. My style was to react firmly and with facts which I expressed calmly without losing my cool at any time. Although I was aware of this man's reputation for a bad temper, I had never really seen him in action. Witnessing him acting as a hysterical maniac over an insignificant procedural issue made me see him as insecure and lesser of a man. I was in control, he was not. How embarrassing it must have been for him not too long after when his wave of anger had subsided, to have to come to me with a personal problem whose solution was in my hands. I surprised him by assisting him without taking advantage to remind him of the ill will he had created in me with his prior irate behavior. Instead, I chose to teach him a lesson by continuing to be the same cool person he had offended and not to allow the memory of his unpleasant reaction embitter me.

Another incident that stands out in my mind as a perfect example of how anger can minimize a person's stature occurred with a girl with which I worked very closely. She had a possible piece of business to one of our hotels and had developed a close relationship with the decision maker. Our boss, totally unaware of how much this account meant to her, decided to make follow-up calls and called on the account. When he reported to her the negative results he had obtained, she turned on him blindly infuriated to the point of crying, losing sight of the unimportance of the matter, if properly evaluated. The boss was at a loss as to what was occurring and could not understand the reason for her violent reaction. Luckily for her, he was not a quick-tempered person and did not react harshly, as he could have, which would have added to her problem—a problem she created unnecessarily. Instead, he tried to reason with her to make her understand he had no intention to interfere with her efforts. Once she calmed down, she confessed how ashamed she was at her behavior, realizing how wrong she had been in reacting so childishly. Unfortunately, the damage was done, and she could not go back on the bad moments she had put herself through as well as others. It would have been so much simpler and better for all if she had taken control of herself and realized that her supervisor had merely acted in good faith with no ulterior motives. She could have firmly but calmly stated to him that in the future she preferred he would allow her to do her own follow-ups up on her accounts based on her closer and better personal rapport. Had she handled the problem in this manner and kept her cool, she would have made a strong and clear statement and would have avoided the childish incident that reflected so poorly on her as a person.

I have strongly defended my position on occasions, but only when the matter merited taking a firm stand because of its significance and because it could affect me in an important way. Anything short of this, I have learned to handle in a cool and unaffected manner. I have convinced myself and disciplined myself on this attitude so that I really am not suppressing any hostile feelings when I brush off an unimportant incident instead of getting upset.

I do not like to be controversial or opinionated during brief and casual encounters. I feel I have my own convictions and have learned that accepting another person's position during such times is not going to alter mine nor will I be able to alter theirs, if I tried. So, why waste energy and time and get all worked up when time could be better spent in pleasant amiable uncontroversial conversation which leaves everyone in better spirits. I will not argue about religion, politics, morals, and any controversial subject during social get-togethers when it is evident to me that I will not accomplish anything but misuse precious time intended for pleasant chit-chat.

I recall attending a command performance cocktail party where I had never met any of the attendees, nor would I ever see them again in all probability. Time was spent in small talk with some and a general exchange of pleasantries with everyone. We would be at the party for only a couple of hours at the most so there was no purpose in entering into any other kind of conversation. However, there was one man who did his best to get me involved in two controversial subjects—-injustice to blacks in the South and capital punishment. I succeeded in not expressing any strong opinions on either. It simply was not my intention to get into any kind of debate with a person whom I had just met, whom I would probably never see again, and who obviously cherished arguing if he would risk spoiling brief moments of enjoyment by bringing up issues of that nature. I knew nothing would be gained by expressing a strong opinion, contrary to his, because I would certainly not have changed his thinking. I would just have allowed myself to have been lured into the trap of an unpopular chronic debater who thrived on arguing, and it was best to tactfully move on to more enjoyable and congenial company.

I refuse to participate in discussions concerning decor and grooming because these are subjects that are dear to everyone's heart, and most people consider they have good taste in these areas and are partial to their taste selection. We should all decorate our surroundings and dress as we see best. Although we are each entitled to our own particular taste, we should recognize there are many ways of creating, presenting and perceiving beauty.

Unless you are taking part in an official debate or acting as an authority on a particular subject, opinions should be stated in such a way so as to avoid futile arguments by rephrasing your statements with remarks like, "I may be wrong but" or "I am not an authority on these matters, but it seems to me". Whatever your method, the idea is to steer away from confrontation on matters that are not important enough to defend at the expense of getting upset. Definitely, you should keep away from discussions on matters on which everyone is entitled to an opinion and conviction. Certainly you should not engage in discussing confrontational subjects during casual social times when the occasion calls only for small talk, amiable conversation, and good mood.

You will benefit immensely from putting things in perspective to avoid concern and anxiety. Whenever you feel angry or upset, try asking yourself, "Is it really that bad?" Maybe not. If you put things in their proper perspective, you will discover that whatever has made you upset or caused you concern did not warrant losing your valuable peace of mind. So often you lose sleep and worry over matters that are not really that important when evaluated more closely. You can magnify things to such an extent that you see them out of proportion completely. If you can manage to keep things in their true perspective, some upsets can be put aside, and some negative feelings avoided or eliminated. If you are successful in eradicating as many negative feelings from your lives as you can, you will in turn add more happy moments to your lives which is the objective we are all trying to achieve.

I had an experience which worried me for several days until 1 realized how badly out of proportion I had blown what had happened. Driving to work at a street light which I cross every day, I forgot that the sign on the corner read that turns could not be made on red between certain hours. My mind had somehow gone back to an older sign on that corner that had read differently so I made the turn on red although I had seen a police car approaching from the opposite direction. Well, I was stopped and fined $25 which at the time was a steep fine. I was terribly upset with myself because I could have avoided the fine if I had been more careful. Deep inside what was really bothering me was that I had foregone buying a number of things that I really wanted because I felt I should not spend money on unnecessary items. What could be more unnecessary than a $25 fine? This was especially annoying when it had happened only because I had confused the hours on the sign. I could only reason that I had virtually thrown $25 down the drain. This thought obsessed me for a few days. Every time it came to mind, it put a damper on my day. Finally, I forced myself to think of the many truly terrible things that could have happened in my life, far worse than a $25 fine, which could have caused me genuine unhappiness, and not this minor mishap. When I was able to put the $25 fine in its proper place, and realized how many other wonderful things I had in my life for which to be thankful , I concluded: what was a $25 fine, anyway?

When you come down to it, there are relatively few important matters that should cause you true concern as compared to the many unimportant ones you allow to interfere with your happiness. If you and your loved ones enjoy physical, mental, and spiritual health, have love and peace of mind, are productive with fulfilling work, have no great financial problems, and can live in harmony with yourselves and others, I would say that practically any other problem is relatively and comparatively insignificant. It can either be solved or lived with if you put it in its proper perspective. I know this attitude is not easy to master since as frail human beings, we cannot help but be swayed and be thrown by the many currents that besiege us during a lifetime. However, you must at minimum be able to acknowledge that if you have health, love, and peace of mind, most of your other problems are not as devastating as you allow them to be.

You should work at cultivating and conquering the art of being happy when the basic ingredients are present despite the problems that may come your way to temporarily distract you. I have not mastered this attitude entirely, and sometimes I catch myself not living by it. I am working at it and as I do, I am avoiding myself unnecessary worry by putting problems in their proper perspective. You should ask yourself when you feel tormented by problems: "Is it really that bad? What if instead of this problem, something much worse were to happen that I could not solve?" If you can discipline yourself to accept that nothing is ever perfect and that you must have small detours and minor problems in your lives, you will have taken one major step in the right direction to rid yourself of unnecessary concern. You must learn to focus on your many blessings and not on little adversities. You will see how much better you will be able to cope with the small problems that will arise. It will be surprising to see how many things will wipe themselves off from your worry board when you look at them with this attitude.

RULE 11: DON'T BE PETTY. KEEP YOUR COOL AND PUT PROBLEMS IN THEIR PROPER PERSPECTIVE.

CHAPTER 12

Here And Now

Today is the best day of your life. It is here, it is now, it is reality, and you are alive. Tomorrow today will be gone. There is nothing you can do about this except assure yourself that you have lived today to the fullest so you will not have any regrets facing you tomorrow. Don't let today slip out of your hands brooding over what you did or did not do yesterday or worrying about what tomorrow might bring.

Yes, we should plan ahead so that tomorrow, that will soon be our today, can be beautiful too, but not at the expense of sacrificing today. First, you must live today for it cannot be recaptured, and once behind you, it is one day less of life left. But, you have the option to live it fully or to waste it pathetically. It is your choice.

Today may happen to be a very blah Monday, it may be raining or snowing and no sign of apparent excitement in sight, but it still is special because it represents precious time that cannot be relived once it has passed. So, don't kill it! Every today is much too valuable not to be lived as best you can. Granted, all your todays will not be full of interesting things to do or with big happenings, but there are many everyday pleasant occurrences and moments in everyone's life. Perhaps, they may appear insignificant but they can afford you diverse sources of enjoyment and pleasure. You should not take for granted these smaller happenings and moments in your life but learn to grasp them so that each today is a day lived rather than a day in which you merely existed. Here are just a few to get you started:

Who doesn't have a good meal to be enjoyed at home?
Or a nice TV program to watch?
How about hugging your man or woman?
Or playing with your children or watching them at play, or asleep?
A brisk walk can be invigorating.
Reading an interesting book or magazine may meet your fancy.
How about sitting outside and watching a beautiful sunset?
Or maybe you would like browsing through your plants and watching how they thrive?
Playing with your dog or cat is always fun.
You can call a good friend and have a good chat visiting over the phone.
Or maybe you would prefer going shopping?
How about all those snapshots you need to organize and place into albums which will bring back pleasant and good memories?
Or maybe you would just enjoy looking at old photographs which is always fun?
You could bake some cookies which your children will love.
How about treating your coworkers to some good pastry?
You can do some researching online or clean up your email messages.
Today you can try that new hair color you have not dared.
Or give yourself a good manicure and pedicure.
Does catching a good movie on TV appeal to you?
Maybe you can rent a movie you have missed.

And while you are at it, enjoy munching on some hot popcorn, or delight yourself with a luscious chocolate bar. True you might add a pound or two, but tomorrow you can cut down to compensate but enjoy today.

Recognize all of these simple things that exist in everyone's life? They can fill an uneventful day very nicely. And, if on one of those rare occasions you find absolutely nothing in your today that appeals to you, you can still relax and enjoy just being alive. This in itself should stimulate you into appreciating more vividly all that is beautiful around you to enjoy.

I know people who have hardly lived one today of their existence just worrying and providing for tomorrow. While you should plan to some extent for the future, this should be kept within reason. You should not allow planning for the future to become an obsession to the point that all of your todays are spent taking care of your tomorrows. You must enjoy and live today with the conviction that it will never come back. The reality is that no one can assure us there will be a tomorrow —- reality is today. Providing and planning for the future is wise if it can be accomplished without abnormal sacrifice in living today. With some people, living today only to provide for tomorrow becomes such a fixed pattern that even if they had reasonably provided for the future, they still would not feel ready to enjoy today. They probably would go on waiting for that tomorrow that so worries them.

There is an old Spanish Andalusian proverb, "Que me Quiten lo Bailao", which I often recall when I want to do something today rather than wait for tomorrow. This wise Proverb means "Let them take away from me what I have already danced," which, of course, is quite impossible. So dance or live every chance that comes your way. Today you have health, today you are strong, today you are young or you are happy to have lived many good years. Today is so precious, because today you are alive. Tomorrow, this may not be regardless of how much you may prepare for it. I have never waited to do anything one year for the next if I have found a way to accomplish it earlier. I am happy for practicing this here and now principle for I feel I have done a lot of "dancing" that no one can take away from me, just in case I do not have a tomorrow.

Some people have never married because they have not found the right financial conditions to take on this responsibility. This is especially true with men, and they reach old age perhaps with savings but alone without a family and with little created. Many people will not take a vacation or do anything that requires major financial expenditure because "things are bad." These people will always think that things are not good. They will procrastinate in the name of tomorrow's security for fear of being caught unprepared. This can become a way of life with some people, and they will go on killing their todays day after day until death arrives without having lived. They may reach tomorrow without the strength, health or desire to do all those things they have been putting off for years waiting for the perfect time.

You have to find the right time in your todays. I am speaking of doing within reason. I am certainly not proposing that you buy yourself a diamond ring or take a trip around the world if you know that tomorrow you will not be able to pay for it, or if you know for a fact that your job is in jeopardy. Extremes are always dangerous, and a middle of the road compromise is the answer. But, I do believe that if today you are enjoying good health, your job appears reasonably secure, and you can manage to put enough together to do something you really would enjoy and still be able to meet your obligations tomorrow, even at reasonable sacrifice tomorrow, you should not hesitate to do it today. If you stop to think of all the horrible things that could happen tomorrow, you will never enjoy any of your todays. What is more, those horrible things created by a pessimistic attitude rather than by concrete facts, will probably never happen, but you will never be able to turn the clock back on all of the todays you missed and lost.

Things have a way of shaping up, and when one door closes, another one opens for you, so do not live life in constant fear in anticipation of tomorrow. The only fear you should have is that of not having lived today because you cannot do much about this once it is gone.

I know a man who has existed his entire life fearing what tomorrow would bring and preparing for every eventuality. He married late, not because he was living an exciting bachelor life, but because of his gutless assessment that "things were rough" and it was impossible to assume the financial responsibility marriage represented. As a result, he had no children because he had married too late to start a family, already cheating himself of the immense joy and pride a man experiences as a father. This man goes about his lonely existence with very meager and scarce pleasant memories. He does not buy clothes, he does not travel, and he is certain times are getting worse each day, but he will be ready. Yes, he will be ready —- ready to die tomorrow without ever having lived. This man's problem has been one primarily of fear of economic insecurity.

Economic insecurity is not the only reason that holds people back from living today, although it is probably one of the strongest. Sometimes, people do not live today because they become habitual procrastinators as if they had an exclusive claim on time and it belonged to them permanently. These people think there will always be time tomorrow to do whatever they really feel like doing today. If they could kick this habit, they would enjoy so much more today. Others just suffer from general insecurity, fearing everything so they dare not make a move today. They are afraid to go on vacation because they could have an accident or get sick in a foreign country, or their house could be burglarized while they are away. They cannot leave their pets or plants unattended so they decide it is better to stay home. They really would like to go to the beach today, but it is a bit cloudy, and they might be caught in the rain and catch a cold, or they might get trapped in heavy traffic getting back, so better leave it for some other day. Whatever their reasons, these people exist in a state of fear that prevents them from living today.

Then there are people who live such responsible lives they do not allow themselves the irresponsibility of having fun and doing those things they like. They would like to go to the movies tonight, but it will be so late when they get back that they will be too tired tomorrow for work, so best forget it. What if you are a little tired tomorrow, you will manage, but it certainly is worth risking for the enjoyment you can have today. They would enjoy sitting down to read a good book they have been dying to read, but they just do not have time because the house has to be cleaned, or they have to do whatever other chore they feel must be done first. These responsible slaves habitually feel they do not have the right to enjoy today until they have met all of their duties. Again, like with anything else, this attitude has to be handled with moderation. We all have certain inescapable responsibilities to meet, but we should not become slaves to our responsibilities, so that we cannot enjoy those things we would like to do today. It certainly is not going to hurt anyone to eat a TV dinner or a canned soup with a sandwich once in awhile if by doing this you can give yourself time to go to the beach or to the art show or you are free to do anything else you like. What's wrong with tidying up the house quickly to make it presentable and organized and foregoing a first-class house cleaning job on occasion if the time can be dedicated to doing something you really wish to do today?

As an optimist, I have never feared what tomorrow might bring and have always felt confident that I can handle all my tomorrows. But, I do tend to be the responsible type and have to fight the habit of putting off things I want to do because of certain responsibilities that were truly not that important or necessary. Within reason, I am trying to do everything I would enjoy today by taking shortcuts with chores that can be done in simpler ways and by eliminating the unnecessary ones. In this manner if I don't make it tomorrow, like the old Spanish proverb says "Que me quiten lo bailao."

Whatever you do, do not let any opportunity pass you by because it can be done tomorrow if you can reasonably do it today. Today will never come your way again, and no one holds a guarantee that tomorrow will happen. There is only a today which is here and now.

RULE 12: LIVE TODAY. DO NOT SACRIFICE TODAY WORRYING ABOUT TOMORROW AND REGRETTING YESTERDAY.

CHAPTER 13

Some Rain Must Fall In Everyone's Life – Prayer Is The Answer

There will always be some hurdles to jump and overcome along the way. Life is not a series of pleasant events unfortunately. We all have to face problems from time to time. This is an inevitable part of living, and the sooner we acknowledge and accept this fact, the quicker we will be better able to cope with our difficulties, and our disappointments will appear to be less harsh. We can gain strength from knowing that no difficulty is insurmountable. Many times the alternatives that emanate from solving the problem can actually turn out to be for the best, if you handle the situation with God, optimism and spunk. Even in the darkest of times, when comfort is nowhere in sight, you must always remember that "This too shall pass," continue to pray and hang on. For those who do, most of the time when the bad times have passed and things are rosy again, as they will be, there will be the realization that the problem was not quite as bad as it had appeared.

It is during these rough moments in life when faith in God can give you the strength and hope to bear it out. I do not know how anyone can make it without this faith. I would be totally lost if I thought I was fighting life's battles alone without Him. But, when I talk to my God and ask Him to help me and to show me the way, I know He is listening and that He will help. Why? Because time and time again He has. God works sometimes in strange ways, and his answer sometimes does not come exactly as expected. Later we can always recognize it was His way of helping us and of answering our prayer. Faith will provide the spiritual strength and certainty that the right answer is on its way.

This is what I have learned to be true through time tested experiences. We must pray firmly believing He will give us the solutions we need rather than sitting and fretting at our misfortune. The key to finding the solutions comes from prayer because He does show them in His subtle ways if we ask with faith. When I pray, I talk to God, informally sometimes just as if I were talking to Him face to face so that my prayer is conversation and dialogue. I truly believe He is listening. After praying, you need to look and watch for His signs which He will give you in many ways, and you will be able to identify them if you have faith.

You must be fighters and not give up along the way. Each time you are knocked down, you must jump up and bounce back with renewed strength and more fervent prayer. For me, there is no other way to overcome. If you allow yourself to be defeated, you are losing your right to happiness. Problems are part of the game of living, and we have to have our share of them now and then. However, if through faith we are convinced that our God is near, listening to our pleas, and we have made prayer a daily part of our lives, our problems will be smaller, less frequent, and easier to overcome. My life is living proof of this, and I want to pass this spiritual strength on to you so that you too may be able to weather life's storms knowing that the sun will shine again.

How we handle adversity makes the difference between happy and unhappy people. It is true that some people seem to have more problems than others. My belief is that if we keep in close touch with God and let Him guide us, you will automatically live the kind of life that breeds a minimum of problems, and your misfortunes will be much lighter, further apart, and easier to solve. My own experiences have proven this to be true, and they have strengthened my conviction that prayer is key to a happier life.

Like everyone else, I have had some problems in my life. By comparison, now that they are behind me, they appear minor. When I look at what real tragedy and despair can be, I feel God has spared me, but like everyone else, I have had difficulties to overcome, and moments of distress and concern. Yet, each time the problems have ultimately worked out well which is what matters. My problems have been relatively small and far between. I am convinced this has been because I rap with God every day of my life—not just when I have a problem, but every single day of my life.

It is difficult to convince people, generally speaking, to seek this faith because most everyone associates any talk of God with organized religion. They are quick to brand as a religious freak or a fanatic anyone who speaks of God with blind faith. It is my hope that my words and experiences can reach those who have not found this faith so that they too will find the answers to their problems with God as their partner. I have no particular religion, yet I have grown very close to God. My God is one I can talk to about anything and everything. I can confess my weaknesses to Him and ask Him to understand them and help me overcome them. I am sincere with Him.

I cannot fake with God that I am what I am not because He knows me better than I. This is the God I wish everyone could find because my life is full of experiences that prove that living close to God leads you to the way to happiness.

Here are some of my major challenges during which I prayed desperately with blind faith, and God answered clearly my prayers.

My first major challenge and answered prayer

One of my very first hurdles came up in life before I had attained the deep faith I now have, and sometimes I think God put it in my path so that I would become aware of His existence and power. I was diagnosed at 15 with toxic goiter requiring immediate surgery. In 1946 this was not a simple operation, and many times, surgery could have fatal results or leave the patient suffering for life with much of the pre-surgery symptoms. Even at 15, I was moderately aware of the seriousness of the surgery, and I recall being very worried. I remember staying up late at night so my parents would not see me crying which would have added to their concerns. It was about this time that I began praying and talking to a God I scarcely knew because I came from an atheistic family.

I prayed in my own way entirely self-motivated without prior religious instruction or exposure. All I knew about God and Jesus came from some teachers at school because at the time, limited Christian religion teachings existed at school. We would pray every day "The Lord's Prayer," sang Christmas hymns during the holidays, and some teachers even read from the Bible every day, and we would be read some Old Testament stories so I was slightly familiar with Moses. This was the extent of my religious knowledge. No one encouraged me to pray; I just felt I needed to reach out to a higher power.

Since my faith then was much meeker and practically non-existent, I often wondered why this misfortune had happened to me at such a young age. Now 69 years later, I look back at this episode in my life as something that had to happen so I would learn to seek God in my own way which would gradually bring me greater happiness.

The operation was successful, and I recovered quickly. Afterwards, there was such a turning point in my life that I now know God meant it to happen for good reasons. As a child I had been very active and underweight due to the goiter's effect on my nervous system. After the operation, I became the calm and cool person I have since been. Physically, I became a new person, gaining much needed weight, and even my face reflected a serenity I did not have before. Scholastically, my last year in high school, which was right after surgery, reflected an enhanced and sharper mind with a report card full of A's in every subject.

Surgery was performed in Havana with a world famous surgeon. In 1946, this operation required an intensive pre-surgery treatment while taking a very strong thyroid hormone that could affect the heart if not administered under very special conditions of complete and absolute rest. Because of this it was necessary for me to remain in Havana for four months. It was during this time that Jay and I, summer vacation sweethearts, really got to know each other. We had the time to strengthen our relationship. Prior to these four months, we had just summer puppy love, and although we were so very young, this was the real beginning of the beautiful love affair we have now shared for 66 years. Now, as I analyze what happened, I believe this operation was the way God had planned for us to become closer and to make me healthy. After my surgery my life took a turn for the better in every respect. It was the beginning of a new me.

My second major challenge and answered prayer

Our love that began at 12 and 15 , and its realization in marriage against all odds. (See Chapter 5 –Organize and Act Out your Dreams)

My third challenge and answered prayer

Years later, a major hurdle came our way when Jay found himself involved in a defalcation of company funds as Office Manager of a Cuban Electric Company branch office. He was on the verge of being accused of embezzlement. This was our first major problem that we had to face together, and those days were nightmarish. We could not believe it was happening to us. Jay is an extremely honest person who came from a stock of high integrity people. Suddenly, he was in the midst of a $1000+ defalcation which in the 1950's was a significant amount. At best, he was responsible for the defalcation as Office Manager of the branch where the bills were collected; and at worst, he could be accused of having taken the money. Other than Jay, the only person who had access to the money was his assistant. There was no evidence to prove the assistant was the culprit although his past history and prior record with the company did not speak well of his honesty, and he had similar problems before. In contrast, Jay had an immaculate track record, and company officials appeared to be inclined to not doubt Jay's honesty and to believe that the assistant had misappropriated the funds. However, without concrete proof, the fact remained that the money was missing, and Jay, as Office Manager, was responsible.

This nasty situation lasted a good month between audits and investigations. During those terrible days the only gratifying mitigation was the trust and confidence everyone professed for Jay. At no time was he directly accused of taking the money. Everyone concerned appeared certain that he had no part in it, and the company auditors and other company officials were striving to prove his innocence rather than his guilt. In the end, since there was no evidence to charge the assistant with the embezzlement, Jay was made responsible for allowing the assistant to have access to funds, which was against company policy, hence allowing the misappropriation to happen. He had to reimburse the company for the missing money. To exonerate him in the eyes of everyone, he was reinstated as Manager, and he continued to handle company funds.

When this dreadful problem was going on, I prayed incessantly. As it solved itself, and I look back at the events that followed, I know that God put this problem in our lives for a good reason since nothing but good things resulted from it. Not so for the assistant who eventually lost his job, suffered of poor health, and his life was quite unhappy. What resulted from this passing adversity? Jay had now learned through hard experience that everyone cannot be trusted, and he had to toughen up in this respect. He had trusted his assistant as a friend and had allowed him to handle funds against policy, and for this he paid dearly financially. He also paid in hours of anxiety and distress.

However, he experienced firsthand how rewarding it was to be recognized for his integrity and to witness how well regarded he was among his supervisors, coworkers, family and friends as he went through a situation which pointed directly to him. Only the trust he had earned exonerated him. Ultimately, in a roundabout way the incident brought about an excellent job change for Jay when a short time after he was reinstated, he put in a bid for and won a position within the company which offered a much better position, superior working conditions and growth opportunities. The offices of the new position were located very close to my office so that instead of having to commute for almost two hours each way every day, he was much closer, we rode together, and sometimes went on break together. In all probability, if the problem had not occurred, he might not have considered changing jobs and would not have been exposed to a new facet of work that turned out to be much more challenging and fulfilling.

My fourth major challenge and answered prayer

Then came another major hurdle with Castro's takeover of Cuba, and we saw ourselves unexpectedly living in a communist regime, with freedom threatened, having to leave behind our new home, our good and stable jobs, and the nice lifestyle we had created for ourselves for years. We were compelled to start a new life. Here again, God was with us all the way and helped us through these stressful and difficult times in a most incredible way.

By this time, my faith had grown considerably with each answered prayer. This is the first time that I actually saw God's answer to my prayers almost instantly and absolutely clear. Leaving what we had created was a hard decision for us. Although we were both convinced that Castro was a Communist, it just did not make any sense that a Communist regime would be allowed to survive 90 miles off U.S. shores so we were certain the takeover would not last. Since we were not initially affected, our decision to leave was a cold one. A decision of this magnitude is very difficult to reach when you are unable to visualize clearly an outcome. When circumstances force you to make a decision, you are compelled to act, and the determination becomes logical and inevitable. However, when you must make your decision based on pure expectation, there is much uncertainty and fear, especially when the decision means leaving your first home, good jobs, and a happy life.

Most of 1959 transpired debating on whether or not to leave before things got worse. Jay was very much for leaving, and I wanted to wait, just in case the revolutionary regime was overthrown. In the meantime, the situation worsened, and we did not like what we saw, and feared what was to come. We were young adults who had never lived through a revolution, and knew of communism only from books. Although not yet directly affected, Jay had insisted we should leave mid 1959, and I owe it to him that he pushed me to start thinking of leaving Cuba as a realistic option.

As I detailed in a previous chapter, we did leave Cuba in a miraculous way. After much prayer, God gave me a clear and irrefutable sign that led me to reach the right decision. And, all that followed after that sign made our exodus safe and perfect with everything we needed to start our new life in the U.S.

We began the long drawn out process to leave Cuba in October 1959 which included trying to get all our possessions out of the country as well as our money, and Jay's resident visa. None of this was easy, but God was with us. My boss fought for us, got my transfer to PanAm Miami with seniority honored, and our money out of Cuba. In the midst of all this, I almost lost my U.S. citizenship due to a technicality and a new law. This was another major hurdle to overcome since my citizenship was the basis for everything, including Jay's resident visa. By this time, the American Embassy in Havana was packed with Cubans trying to get resident visas to leave, and things just did not move fast. Again, my boss went to bat for us with the Embassy Naval Attaché who was a close personal friend, and after several weeks, the State Department ruled in my favor, and my U.S. citizenship was reinstated.

It was mid-December when at times I was still tormented with indecision and uncertainty as to whether we were making the right move. Lying in bed one evening, feeling rather miserable because of a wisdom tooth extraction earlier that day, I talked to God in that very special way that only happens when you are desperate. I asked Him to show me the way and to help us with our decision. Should we leave as quickly as possible or should we wait to see if the revolutionary government was toppled. I asked fervently for a clear sign. Just a few minutes elapsed when I heard the front door bell. Waiting several minutes to find out who had arrived, I got up and peeked. To my total shock, I saw my living room literally invaded by a group of militiamen and women, loaded with machine guns. I felt such terror at the spectacle before me that I could hardly move or speak. They were searching all through the house for some kind of evidence or excuse to take Jay into custody. Apparently we had been accused of being counter revolutionaries with close ties to exiles. All of a sudden I saw before me a clear picture of what Cuba would become and what our lives would be if we stayed. I was certain that this was God's answer, loud, clear, and immediate. I had asked for a sign; there it was.

From that moment forward, I never faltered. I had a quick glimpse into the future of Cuba, and I was sure we wanted out. Our pretty home and stable jobs lost importance when personal freedom was at stake. I was totally sure then we had made the right decision, and all that occurred afterwards proved it beyond a doubt.

Definitely, this was an important crossroad that changed our lives in so many ways —- but all for better. I know that God watched over us at that crossroad and led us to safety and a better life. I know He did this because I prayed fervently and with immense faith that evening. So many wonderful things happened to us since —- like a chain reaction. What seemed to be a horrible setback when it was occurring, I now know happened to us for the best. Because we acted quickly, as soon as we recognized the Lord's sign, quite ahead of most, both Americans and Cubans, we were able to ship to Miami all our belongings, including our house effects, photograph albums, and even my piano. Eight large crates full of precious belongings went out on a PanAm cargo plane one evening, and a few days later, the Communist government decreed that all shipments of personal belongings of U.S citizens returning home would be stopped. No more shipments were allowed. It appeared as if we would just make each door before it closed behind us. We made it each stage of the way, and finally left Cuba early March 1960, leaving behind what we had created during years, but this was the start of a new life that would bring us much more happiness.

At this point, it is important to note and observe how God works, and it is not until much later that the entire picture became visible. Years before during my first year as a secretary in PanAm Havana, a number of things happened that affected my later life in a very miraculous way. The reason why I was working for the man who helped us in such an unbelievable way dated back to eight years before when I was asked to fill in for his then secretary who was suddenly taken seriously ill and would possibly not return. At the time, I had just joined the airline in Havana, was 20 years old, just a very junior secretary that had never even met Warren Pine, PanAm's top executive in Havana. I did nothing to get this assignment. I had only done my job and tried to win everyone's good will and respect. Why me? There were many other secretaries with much more seniority and experience than I that could have been assigned to this top secretarial job. Yet, the man for whom I was working for less than a year, to my amazement and awe, found it in his heart to recommend me for the position because he believed I was the best qualified. He did this even though it was disruptive to him because he had to find another secretary to replace me. However, he evaluated it unselfishly as a great opportunity for me and was certain I was the best person for the position. Luck or miracle?

This temporary position, as I explained in a previous Chapter, became permanent through the years, and eight years later, the man I with whom I was assigned to work was the man who had in his hands the ability to do for me all the remarkable things that he did. I was the only PanAm employee from Havana to be transferred to PanAm Miami with full seniority. God blessed us even further because this seniority in later years gave me the 30 years of service for which I now have a nice pension. One occurrence led to the other. I did not plan any of it. I did not to try to displace anyone. All I did during those years was to be the best I could be, have faith in the Lord, pray to acknowledge his existence and power, and Let Go, Let God.

We arrived in Miami with little cash and just my PanAm job, homeless, carless, and confused. However, we were much more fortunate than those that followed later in the massive exodus of Americans and Cubans that occurred during the ensuing years. Many had to leave with just a prescribed number of clothing, no cash, and arrived in this country jobless, with a language barrier, and having to start their lives over again. My North American boss who helped us so much had his Havana apartment frozen by the Communist government with all of his belongings inside and lost everything when he left.

I see all of this as the first palpable proof God had given me of his existence and that He was there ready to help if we just knocked at His door. I know that if I had not prayed the way I did that evening,

God's signs would not have appeared as clearly as they did, and I would have probably influenced Jay to wait a bit longer hoping things would improve. None of the good things that happened to us would have come to be as they did.

My fifth major challenge and answered prayer

Now in Miami we faced new problems. Jay needed to find a job in a city that came to life only with winter tourism, had practically no industry and offered little in the way of jobs the rest of the year. A jobless man is a very unhappy and depressed man—especially when he watches his wife leave each morning for work. Most men consider themselves the primary providers and are humiliated when the opposite occurs. At first, Jay was very hopeful that the jobless situation would not last long, and he optimistically searched the newspaper each day for job ads. Jobs were scarce in Miami in 1960, and the situation was aggravated by the fact that he was a foreigner who did not master the language. My poor husband struggled every day, dropping me off at work, and facing the jobless challenge. The first opportunity that developed was a shoe salesman job on commission in a downtown shoe store. This was not the type of work he had hoped for, but nonetheless a job, so he did what he had to do.

A friend of our Miami family had promised help in getting him a city bus driver job for the City Transit Line, but this would not materialize immediately. He would have to wait. After almost two months of job hunting he was losing spirit and having doubts as to whether he should have left Cuba and his good job. About this time, one morning as I left our small one-room efficiency, while our new house was being built, I encouraged Jay to again call on an ex-PanAm friend working for a small airline. Because he had contacted my friend when we first arrived, he did not want to pester the man. I did not agree and reasoned that it had been already two months since he had spoken to him. After all, it was not my friend who needed the job so he had no personal reason to be on top of our problem. I believed it was time for a reminder, just in case, but Jay did not agree.

With these troubling thoughts in my mind, I was unable to concentrate at the office. All that came to mind was the sad man I had left behind. Although I am an optimist, I too began to wonder if maybe our lives had made a turn for the worse, and perhaps things were never going to get better. We had committed ourselves with a nominal down to buy a home, and this meant that come May, we would be faced with a mortgage payment we could barely make with just my salary. When we arrived in March, the month of May seemed so far away, and we were sure that in this land of opportunities, Jay would do well quickly. He was a hard worker, strong, young, healthy and willing to work at whatever came his way. May was just days away and there was nothing promising in the horizon. As all of these negative thoughts ran through my mind, I had to leave my desk for the lounge to have a few solitary moments. My heart turned to God as it always had in the past when faced with serious problems. This time my prayer was not the usual every day prayer. It was a desperate call for help. When I returned to my desk, I felt much more at peace with a new surge of hope.

Not much longer after getting back to my desk, the phone rang, and on the other side of the line was an excited and happy man who after all had decided to see my friend at the small airline despite what he had told me that morning. The timing had been perfect. They were looking for someone for the Accounting department to start working right away. He had favorably impressed the Accounting Manager, and the job was his. This was April 27, 1960, and we were scheduled to close on our house and move in three days later on May 1. What timing! Had he not gone to see our friend that day, he would have missed out, but God made me encourage him to go and moved him to pursue it. Seems like a fairy tale miracle? Well, it happened to us in this real world. I just know God heard my plea in the lounge as he did in Cuba that evening, and as he has done many other times since.

This was not just an ordinary accounting job—it was the start of Jay's airline career which fulfilled him totally and opened new horizons for him and the entire family, giving him tremendous opportunities to grow in the industry, to travel, to meet new people and to be exposed to almost every facet of an airline operation. It opened a whole new world for both of us and our family that otherwise would not have happened. He learned the various phases of an airline operation, ranging from Accounting, Reservations, Airport, to finally Sales and Marketing for which he was a natural with his outgoing likeable personality. He held various important Sales Manager positions in different airlines for over 20 years.

When we look back, again I see God's hand at this turning point in our lives because the bus driver job that had been a possibility when Jay was jobless did materialize after he was already working with the airline. The bus driver job paid substantially more than the airline position and offered greater security because the Miami Transit Line was a well-established company as compared to a small Latin American airline operation. When the driver job became available and offered to Jay, we both rapped with God and asked Him not to allow him to become confused in this important decision. After talking to his new boss, he encouraged him to stay with them. He believed he had a better future with them than with the transit line, and Jay decided to stay. He had seen God's signs clearly: he was happy with his work and God had put the airline job in his path first. Two months later, the transit line was hit with a general strike that lasted for months. When it was finally settled, all the striking employees, including our friend, lost their jobs, and only new employees remained. We knew then once more that God had helped Jay make the right decision at this crossroad.

My sixth major challenge and answered prayer

When I reported to the PanAm Executive Offices on our arrival from Havana, I was immediately greeted by Bill Raven, the Assistant Division Manager, who much to everyone's surprise went out of his way to welcome me with a big hug. This man was notorious for being unfriendly and detached, and this display of affection appeared quite unusual to the staff. However, again years before in Havana unplanned things had happened to me that would later open doors for me. When I had just begun with PanAm in Havana, I had been assigned to work with Raven for a few days during a visit to Havana. After, on numerous occasions while I was working with Warren Pine, he had also visited our offices, and I had helped him and his family with passport renewals at the American Embassy. Evidently, he recalled me well, and was happy to have me join the Miami PanAm family. As I have stated before, God has a plan of his own, and when you just do your best and leave the rest to Him, He works in such a way that if you had planned and premeditated with utmost care, intelligence, and precision for a similar outcome, it would possibly never happen. This was exactly the case when scarcely a month after working at the Miami Executive offices to cover vacations, I was approved to take a month vacation I was owed before summer vacations began. This month vacation came in just perfect to move in to our new house on May 1. It was during this vacation month that Bill Raven called to ask me to work with him as his secretary on my return on June 1 because he had just fired his girl. This was quite an unexpected promotion in less than two months—from floater to administrative assistant to the Division's Assistant Manager! Once more, looking back, God's plan was at work. Had I not been assigned to work with this man years before in Havana, and continued to have dealt with him during my Havana days, and had he not had a problem with his secretary, this break for me would have never happened. But, like magic, it did!

Now Jay's job hurdle had been overcome, and I was about to begin a new challenging job. It seemed as if we were again on the road to stability with everything in its place: our new house, our daughter Adele who had been with my parents in Tampa while we got settled was now back with us, and my mother would be staying with us to help care for her. Everything had fallen into place perfectly, right? Not quite so, because my enticing promotion brought difficulties with it.

I soon discovered that working for Raven was not going to be easy, and this hurdle was an entirely new one for me. He was a difficult man. Nothing I had learned or thought I had mastered in people skills had equipped me to deal with a person like him. He was an abusive despot and an insecure bully who kept everyone in his staff on pins and needles. Almost simultaneously with my acceptance of the position, he was appointed Division Manager pro tem of PanAm's Latin American Division with three months to prove himself. This was a most important position for him, and the challenge added another dimension to the job. He was relentless in his drive and went into second gear to prove beyond a doubt that he was totally capable to handle the position. His already intolerable disposition worsened. The tension was intense. Looking back, there was a lesson to be learned for me from this experience at age 30. I needed to toughen up. No longer was I dealing with a normal gentleman-like man like my school professors, other bosses, my husband or my father whom I knew exactly how to manage.

My Havana ex-boss, Warren Pine, told me when I accepted the position that perhaps I had met my Waterloo, and I began to believe it. My soft spoken, easy going, diplomatic characteristics irritated Raven instead of pleasing him. He viewed these traits as signs of weakness, and he had no respect for weakness. It took a while, much prayer, support from the girl that was assigned to help me, before I was able to change and to conquer the feeling of inadequacy he had instilled in me.

I began to see him for what he truly was—a terribly insecure man masquerading his own sense of inadequacy with a bully front. Once the Lord gave me the insight to the problem and strengthened my own character, I stopped fearing him and asserted myself forcefully much to his surprise. Contrary to everything I had been taught or believed in, I stopped projecting modesty or humility and instead boasted about my abilities. Normally, I would never have followed this kind of behavior, but it worked, and our relationship began to change. In this odd and different manner, I won his respect. This tough man, who no one was able to handle and who took advantage of his position with all his immediate staff, now knew that I was no longer afraid of him and that I knew I was capable of performing my job well. He began to look upon me for advice and help. I had removed the obstacles.

At that point I had learned that sometimes there are different rules in dealing with different people, and what normally works with most people does not necessarily function with others who have deep personality flaws. I fearlessly and without a shadow of modesty projected and displayed a stronger approach showing him my capabilities in many areas that were important to him like speech writing, handling his expense reports, and with my diplomatic attributes, managing and screening his team of 12 department heads efficiently. My behavior convinced him I was the person he needed next to him, and I knew then I had the upper hand. He showed me admiration and praised my efforts. I had stood up to him, and he had fallen back. There were many ups and downs in the relationship, but in the end, I became his right hand, and we worked congenially for 12 years until he was forced to retire after 40 years of service. In fact, we remained friends for many years after his retirement. God showed me a new lesson, and this hurdle disappeared.

For some years our lives rolled on smoothly and happily without any major crises. We had our second child, Annette, a beautiful baby that brought us much joy. We traveled, progressed in our jobs, made friends, and watched our oldest daughter become an attractive and intelligent young lady. Things could not be better, but then 12 years later another hurdle came my way.

My seventh major challenge and answered prayer

At the time, Bill Raven had been appointed Vice President and I was his Administrative Assistant with a chunky salary in those days. I had years with the company and was enjoying my prestigious and challenging position. Panam was having serious economic troubles, and administrative reorganizations were the order of the day. Top Management decided to abolish our entire department and retire Raven, and my job became nonexistent. Although I knew I would probably not have much difficulty finding a job, especially with my bilingual ability, it was frightening after having been with one company for years to start over again elsewhere. Besides, the travel business itself fascinated me, and I loved it. I could not visualize myself working for an attorney or an insurance or mortgage company. My boss gave me an excellent recommendation letter for another major airline in the area, and I was offered a job, but the salary was half my PanAm salary. I went to many interviews and had numerous job offers outside the travel field, but salary in every case was much less than my PanAm salary. I finally reconciled to the idea that it would not be possible to find a job starting with a comparable salary to what I was accustomed. Although I was already willing to accept a significant cut, I was confused as to which position to accept.

As usual, as I approached an important crossroad, I prayed more than ever. I had a special talk with God with that same deep faith I have felt at other important crossroads. I had done the groundwork. I had gone to the interviews and had sold myself, but now I needed His higher power to help me choose what was best. I was in His hands. A few days later, like magic again, I received a call that Inter-Continental Hotels, PanAm's wholly owned hotel subsidiary, was opening a new Sales office in Miami, and the new Sales Director was interested in me. Salary, although still below my PanAm salary, was much closer to it. I was definitely interested and would be willing to accept a smaller cut. There were definite advantages to this job because my 21 years' seniority would be recognized which meant that immediately I would be eligible for five weeks' vacation which would never happen in any other organization as a newcomer. I accepted Inter-Continental Hotels' offer and was hired. I was happy with my decision in many ways. I would still be in the travel business which I so loved, I would be working in the same building, surrounded by the same familiar faces, and even the work itself had certain similarities as both companies operated with the same policies and procedures and used the same communications system. Since I had travel privileges through Jay, now I could couple these with the hotel privileges for our trips. Sounds perfect? Not quite, there was one more hurdle to jump.

I had received a lump sum severance pay from PanAm, but since Inter-Continental and PanAm funds were considered one and the same, policy called for me to return the severance money. This was impossible. I had used most of the money in paying bills and on house improvements, and this was not what I had anticipated when I accepted the job. At no time had I been told this would be a condition for accepting the position. Again, indecision and concern took over. Should I stay and pay the money back or should I take a job elsewhere? I enlisted help from my two ex-bosses, Pine and Raven, to intercede with PanAm and Inter-Continental in my behalf in waiving this requirement, but even though they offered practical solutions to Inter-Continental Management which could have circumvented the policy requirement, these were rejected, and I found the battle was mine alone to fight.

Always asking for guidance from above, I was inspired to make one last effort of my own. I wrote directly to PanAm's top Management in New York appealing to them as a loyal 21-year employee and expressing my surprise and disappointment with the unfairness of asking me to return the money when I had not been told beforehand of this requirement. The letter brought results, and I was offered the opportunity to return the money at $100 a month which was only a partial solution because now it would further cut my salary. Initially, I was not sure whether I wanted to accept this. I was given two weeks for a decision or be terminated.

Confused and sick with the flu at home a few days before I had to make my decision, I shared the problem with God and asked for his help in clearing my confusion. The fever put me to sleep after praying, and in a half awake state, I clearly saw what I should do. When I awoke, I was very tranquil and at peace. How could I have been so confused when it was all so clear? I should stay with Inter-Continental Hotels. Even with the salary cut, my salary was much higher than what was being offered by outside firms. I would not have any seniority with an outside firm and only 2 weeks' vacation at the most. I would definitely be much happier with Inter-Continental because I would still be in the travel business, and I would still be part of PanAm. None of these benefits would exist in any other job. The indecision was over. I decided to stay. The answer to my prayer was immediate and clear.

I know that God had shown me clearly in my dream what I should do because during the ten years that followed I received many salary increases that brought my salary to an attractive level again. I enjoyed many wonderful benefits and thoroughly enjoyed my sales position. I was able to take advantage of complimentary hotel facilities around the world that were offered only to sales personnel for familiarization purposes for the purpose of doing a better selling job of our numerous hotels. With the years my vacation time was increased to 6 weeks, and with Jay's travel benefits and Inter-Continental's travel allowance afforded to sales personnel to visit hotels, we had a perfect combination that made possible many beautiful trips we could never have afforded under normal circumstances.

Additionally, because my 21 years with PanAm were recognized, I was able to complete 30 years and became vested. As a result, I now enjoy a nice pension. What more could I have asked?

When I look back I see that God had given me clear signs to take the Inter-Continental Hotels job. The job was offered to me, the other jobs I had sought, the Inter-Continental job had fallen on my laps as if from heaven itself.

I know God has always been with us because we have prayed and asked for his help with absolute faith, and every time, we have faced a challenge or a crossroad, his answer has been clear, quick, and has brought better results than that for which we had prayed. It was always His plan. We prayed, watched for the signs, followed them even when sometimes they may not have appeared logical to unbelievers, but in the end they led us to much happiness.

My eighth challenge and answered prayer

Sometime between ages 40 and 50, give or take, couples can be faced with a passing storm for which they should be prepared. At that time some men will undergo a marked crisis. It can be called male menopause or midlife crisis, but call it as you may, it can happen and both husband and wife should be ready for it. This is an entirely psychological crisis which has nothing to do with the man's male virility. It is a time when a man evaluates his life realizing that he has lived more years than probably the years he has left to live, and suddenly he is faced with the reality that he will probably not accomplish all his dreams. He begins to have regrets about not having done many things his way. Hence, he wants to live more selfishly now that he realizes his time is running short.

This crisis hits a man differently depending on two important factors: his own emotional makeup and his assessment of how well he considers he lived the years before. There are also different kinds of men, and therefore, the crisis manifests itself accordingly.

- The easy-going content type man, who does not demand too much from life and is capable of being happy with the small things of life, will probably have fewer symptoms, or they may be so undetectable, that his wife may never sense them.
- The man who lived an egotistical life, doing mainly what he wanted most of the time, without much or any efforts to compromise with his wife, will also probably show very light symptoms. He did all that he wanted without regard to the needs of his wife or family so he did not have regrets.

But, in contrast, you can expect a probable major crisis sometime for these types:

- The man whose emotional makeup makes him demanding of life, who has always dreamed of exciting adventures and feats, and who cannot find fulfillment easily in the small things of life, or
- The man who has compromised a great deal to make his wife and family happy, ignoring his own selfish desires.

I know because Jay was both of the above rolled into one.

At 41 I had read very little about male menopause. The term amused me, and I viewed male menopause as more myth than truth. I regarded the subject as humorous, very remote from my life, and I was certain it would never happen to my man. The crisis came upon us like an unexpected phantom that began to tear our marriage and us individually.

I believe few women in their thirties are aware of what could await them in the next decade regardless of how happy the marriage may be. Consequently, they are totally unprepared, as I was, to cope with this problem when it strikes. As a result, frequently the marriage disintegrates. Often we hear of divorces that occur after 20 years of marriage, and of the fortyish-old man who left his wife of 20 or more years for a younger woman. Everyone feels the unfairness for the wife, but actually it was the wife's lack of understanding of her husband's mid-year problem that provoked the marriage breakdown. Wives need to learn what can be done to help their husbands during these turbulent times and to reach out with more love and wisdom than ever. During this time wives must keep especially appealing physically and sexually for their maturing husbands. I always thought that couples who had 20 years of marriage could begin to relax and just enjoy each other's company without major conflicts and with good passive love. This is far from the truth. As a starter, when you marry young, as we did, you arrive at 20 years of marriage at still a young age. We were 41and 44 . A man of 44 is still sexually active, looks attractive, and still has a lot of living to do. Even though there may be 20 years of life invested in the relationship, the wife is still challenged to keep up and make his life exciting and interesting perhaps, even more than 15 or 20 years before when nothing more was needed but youth. Now wives must be resourceful and work at the marriage with greater imagination.

Jay was 44 when I first noticed him withdrawn and depressed. Thank God, our communications lines were open, and after some probing and a series of profound discussions, all kinds of unhappy feelings began to emerge from him. He confessed he was terribly unhappy. I could glean his concern with age and how little time he had left to live and to do all the things he wanted. I learned of his many regrets. He told me of his desire to become more selfish and to live more for himself. I was shocked. My rock of Gibraltar had crumbled.

Unhappy, I reasoned, what about? What more could he possibly want out of life? I thought we had everything: love, health, family, good jobs. But, I was looking at our lives solely from my standpoint. At first, I thought he was so wrong and unfair. I began to pray more and to read more. As I did, I learned that my husband was a typical case of male menopause with all of the characteristics and symptoms. With this insight, I decided to change my tactics. Instead of blaming him, I searched myself for areas in which I might not have fulfilled him as I should have and in which I could use improvement. I tried to make our life together more interesting and less routine-like by introducing new stimulants in every way I could from small outings, to longer trips, from surprise menus to provocative nightgowns. I interfered less with his freedom and let him appreciate for himself how much more he had within the marriage than outside of it.

My husband has always had to travel frequently on business, and I knew that my 360 degree change was producing results when on one of his trips, he came home one full day earlier than expected and told me he had hurried up his work so he could be back sooner because he had missed me very much. I thank God every day for allowing me to realize what was happening to my husband and for helping me evolve with him. It took me about one year before I sensed I had made real progress, and about two years to feel I had succeeded completely because Jay was again a happy man. My husband has thanked me many times for having held on and having understood his feelings rather than condemning him. He is very appreciative for my actually putting forth efforts to help restore him back to happiness. It was a real challenge, and today I know our marriage was revitalized by what happened. We have a revived love affair.

Because of my own experience, I am concerned about other couples who may be going through this stage in their marriage, or who will be going through it in the future, totally unprepared as I was. I wish I could reach them with this message so that they may be able to save their marriage during this trying time in the marital relationship. I do not have a set of fixed rules or principles on how to help your man during this time of turmoil because each man and each marriage has a makeup of its own, and the crisis can manifest itself strongly or not so strongly. I suggest that every woman in her thirties and certainly before reaching age 40 become cognizant of male menopause and prepare herself as much as possible to detect the condition and learn how to cope with it.

My own experience in a nutshell: it took much love, patience, awareness, intelligence, introspection and re-evaluation of myself, as well as the ability to conquer foolish pride and to change and grow to keep it together during this phase of marriage in the autumn years. It is a tremendous challenge, but is it not worth meeting? I would say it is a resounding YES!

My ninth challenge and answered prayer

When my daughter Adele became a more mature young lady at 19, although apparently leading a happy life, I could sense, she was becoming restless, searching for something deeper than dates and fun. She had a terrific time during her teen years dating and with much boy attention. She was popular both with the girls and guys, had traveled, was in Junior College, worked as a Girl Friday for an insurance agent, and kept busy with much social activity. It all seemed perfect, but I could tell she was now yearning for deeper values that all this activity could not fulfill. I had always wished for her the happiness I had found through love and marriage, and maybe I had instilled in her those values. Maybe, because she had seen our happy marriage close up, she knew a good marriage was not just a myth but really existed. It was evident to me that as she matured, superficial values gave way to deeper ones. Whatever the reason, I knew all of the dating and phone calls were not fulfilling her. In my prayers, I had always asked that some day at the right time she would find the right man, just as I had found her Dad, who would love, admire, and respect her and for whom she would have the same feelings.

The holidays were upon us, and I was planning our usual Christmas party. I was at the hairdressers the day before the party with this concern for my daughter in my mind, and my eyes turned to the wall in front of me. Staring right at me was a picture of the Sacred Heart of Jesus. I was moved to pray for Adele in my customary special way when I have a deep concern. I talked to Jesus as if I were talking to my own father and opened my heart to Him with all of my motherly concern for Adele. I became so emotional that I had to wipe the tears.

The morning following the party she had to babysit for her boss and asked me to be sure to give her phone to anyone who called. About mid-morning the phone rang, and it was Stan, a very nice young man she had dated in high school, and had liked very much. He had been away in college, and they had lost touch, but he was spending Christmas at home, had seen Adele several days before, and evidently the spark was still there when he decided to call her again. One happy and excited girl called to tell me that Stan had asked her to Christmas Eve dinner at his parents' home which she had accepted and they would later come over for our later dinner at home. Well, that was the beginning of a beautiful romance.

They became engaged the following Christmas and married eight months later in August. She never could have found a better man than Stan had she waited until 100. To us he is the son we never had. He's a hard-working, affectionate, aggressive man, and they now have 41years of marriage. They had two sons who now have their own families, and are very loving and special grandsons. Again, God had come through for me. With each living proof my faith has continued to grow. I only wish I could reach others so that they too could find this beautiful source of happiness that is ours just for the asking.

My tenth challenge and answered prayer

A few years later there was more rain in the horizon. Jay developed a nervous stomach which caused him severe discomfort. He was checked and rechecked by doctors and specialists, but the tests revealed nothing. He became very depressed and did not want to participate in any fun activities. When the doctors insisted there was nothing wrong with him, he would not accept that perhaps all his symptoms were being caused by depression. These were rough times for all of us. All the family fun was gone. Our youngest daughter, Annette, felt the brunt of his depression sharply, and it was difficult for her to understand why her fun loving Dad was no more. Luckily, the problem never affected his work, but at home, we felt it very keenly. My normally jovial husband became more sullen each day. Since everything he ate did not agree with him, he lost over 25 pounds. As the condition worsened my appeal to the Lord for his healing grew more passionate. We had been so happy. We had everything: our girls, our new son, our marriage, our love, our jobs, but this new cloud definitely was hanging low and bringing much rain into our lives. I tried to be encouraging and optimistic, but nothing seemed to lift his spirit.

While driving home from work, after having talked with him over the phone and hearing he did not feel well that afternoon, I tearfully prayed to God with all my heart and soul. I had prayed many times before for Jay and his problem, but somehow it seemed as if this time God would not listen. I asked why He did not hear my plea for Jay as He had always before. I begged and implored of Him to be compassionate and help him get well again. I felt very close to God that afternoon, and like other such times when I have sensed His nearness, the answer came quickly and in His surprising and mysterious way.

A few days later I was making copies at the office and ran into a fellow employee whom I saw almost every day, but we never talked much. Never before had we entered into a personal conversation as we did that morning. Normally we would have made only small talk because he was just an occasional acquaintance at the office, but that morning it was different. Instead, when he asked how I was doing something urged me to tell him that my husband was not doing well and that I was quite concerned. Coincidentally (?), he had suffered of something similar but had improved with a medication prescribed by his doctor. I inquired further about his miracle pill, and immediately recognized the medication to be the same anti-depressant that had been suggested for Jay and which he had refused to take because he was certain he was not depressed. My occasional friend offered to bring me a few pills in an unlabeled bottle so Jay could unknowingly try the medication. I consulted with our doctor who agreed wholeheartedly with the plan. This story ended happily with Jay totally cured. He took the "mystery" pill for years as if it had been medication for a nervous stomach, and the depression lifted completely. It was not until many years after that I confessed the truth to him. More than 40 years have passed, and never again has my husband suffered from depression. Why did I encounter this casual acquaintance at the copier? Why did I open up to him, practically a stranger, and told him of Jay's health problems? Why did he happen to have had the same symptoms? Why did he offer to give me the anti-depressant pills? Does not all of this give you reason to believe in miracles?

My eleventh major challenge and answered prayer

There are times that the Lord shows Himself merely to prove his existence. Jay's faith was weaker than mine. He tends to be a person that needs concrete evidence and analyzes situations using more logic than blind faith. I often prayed for him asking the Lord to enter into his heart, mind and soul so that he would see God in everything as I did.

The answer to this prayer came in a trip to Rio for a few days before continuing on to South Africa. The trip had been planned primarily for Annette who now was approaching fourteen and loved animals dearly. When we arrived in Rio, the tour guide who picked us up at the airport told us that the weather in Rio had been continuously overcast and cloudy for the past two weeks, and the forecast was for the same to continue the next day. Unfortunately, we would not be able to see the Christ at Corcovado the following day on our city tour. I believe God inspired me to say without much thought: "Who knows, maybe it will be sunny." I know I did not say this because I thought I had special powers. I had just spurted it out with optimism. Logic and a strong belief in meteorology made Jay immediately retort: "Do you think you can change weather? This has to do with winds and other weather factors, and we have to accept it." Disregarding his scientific explanation, I impulsively reasserted that I did not care about weather forecast and winds, and if the Lord wanted tomorrow to be a beautiful day, it would be. Lo and behold! The next day when our guide came for us, the day was spectacularly gorgeous without a cloud to be seen. The guide himself was astonished because they had not had a sunny and clear day for weeks. We saw the Christ against a splendorous blue sky and have photographs to prove it. Jay did not know what to say to counter the reality before us. I am certain that God did this to strengthen Jay's faith beyond just science and facts. He did hint that sometimes coincidences and odd things can happen so evidently this proof alone would not be enough.

After a few days in Rio we went to Johannesburg and on to Capetown. It was winter in the southern hemisphere, and on arrival at Capetown, our guide told us to prepare for a cold front that would affect our weather on our tour of the Cape of Good Hope. It would be overcast, windy and cold. Since Jay had not given the Lord full credit for the Rio weather, I again felt the need to say that the weather might not be bad, if He so willed it. Jay laughed at my optimism and told me that the Rio episode had made me think I really had special powers. "Of course not", I responded, "but I do know that if God wants it to be a beautiful day, it will be." Of that I was certain. I added: "Since you are such a skeptic, he may need to show you again." Well, it did happen again. The weather at the Cape was windy but very beautiful. This time, Jay was beyond belief. He did not say much, but I could sense that the Lord had given him a lesson in faith that would forever remain with him. And, it did. He often refers to both experiences and sees both as a sign of God's existence.

My twelfth challenge and answered prayer

A major cloud appeared when my daughter Annette who now was a teenager met the wrong boy who affected her life in so many ways. Annette was the perfect daughter. We were very close, she confided in me with all her girl stories and was a great student. Then this young man who was a school dropout without a job and doing nothing productive came into her life when she was almost 15, She became totally infatuated. Her grades began slipping, she started skipping school, and became disrespectful with us. It was chaos as we tried to find our perfect daughter again. My prayers were desperate pleas. We just could not reach her without getting into a fight. These were tough times for our family. My prayers were answered in different stages, but in retrospect, I see God's hand in every stage.

Stage One of her salvation came with a trip to Mardi Gras in New Orleans, that we insisted she had to accompany us, much against her will. During the trip she met teen sons and daughters of the friends we visited who made her see firsthand how badly her boyfriend measured up against young people who studied and were doing something with their lives. She decided of her own volition to break up with the young man on our return. The signs could not have been clearer. Why did we insist on taking her with us to New Orleans? It would have been much easier to leave her with my parents rather than fight her all the way. Why did our friends have children of their own who took the time to entertain Annette?

The second breakthrough came when she herself asked us to change her from the public high school she was attending in 10th grade to a private school. We did not think at the time this was necessary, but she insisted. We had no idea what school to select, but a casual friend with whom I hardly ever spoke called for some unimportant reason. In the course of the conversation she spoke highly of her daughter's private school and the name stayed with me. I decided to explore the school and decided this would be the right school for her. In this school Annette began a turnaround in her studies, but most important of all, in this school Annette met her husband Oscar now of 33 years, who is our second son. He is a very intelligent and creative artist and musician. They have a very good marriage, and were very good for each other. Oscar is a clean cut, decent young man who rescued her during those turbulent times, and Annette made Oscar bloom into a full man.

Again, the signs and the answer were clear. This would never have happened if Annette had not asked us to change her to a private school nor if the casual friend with whom we hardly ever spoke would not have called and spoken of her daughter's school. The young girl that insisted in being placed in a private school graduated from Florida International University cum laude and now holds an excellent position in the University of Miami. She is a talented, affectionate and wonderful woman who is more of a friend than a daughter. Oscar has been a wonderful influence in her life. They have a beautiful family with a daughter and a son with whom they have a very close relationship and whom we adore. I thank God every day for helping us as He did each step of Annette's comeback. None of what occurred was of our doing—all we did was pray, God did the rest.

My thirteenth challenge and answered prayer

In 1994, we were faced with a real health hurdle when Jay had to undergo open heart surgery with three bypasses. I prayed and prayed, and died a little waiting for the many hours that transpired before the surgeon came out to tell us the surgery had been successful. Jay is a brave man, and showed no fear, but my faith was tested. Until I saw him convalescing at home five days later, only my prayers carried me through. He did recover quickly with no complications.

About three weeks later, before returning to work, Jay wanted to take a short road trip during a long Columbus Day weekend. His surgeon gave him permission but stressed he should avoid any strenuous activity. It was a very hot October day as we drove through Alligator Alley on our way towards the west coast Florida beaches. Right at the point of no return, deep in the Everglades with no service station in sight, and very little cell reception, Jay noticed a thump that reflected we had a flat tire. I could not believe this was happening. He pulled into the first shoulder, and despite my pleas, insisted that he could handle the tire change. The heat was immense. I kept thinking of the surgeon's warning to not engage in strenuous exertion, and I wanted to call AAA rather than risk a problem in the middle of nowhere. When the male ego is at stake, men can be stubborn. He was adamant; he could do it, and I could help him. Me? Help him with tire changing? Not a chance, I thought. Banking on my help in situations of this kind is not very recommendable, but I tried. Of course, the temporary spare I was holding got away from me and was going straight to the canal when I managed to catch it. Praying is what I do, and this was all I could do, fervently. When Jay knelt to change the tire, the bolts on the tire were so tight, he could not unfasten them. He was perspiring heavily, and I was praying just as heavily.

Suddenly, out of nowhere, a van pulled up on the shoulder, and a young man jumped out offering to help. He had been driving from the opposite direction and had seen us and turned around to help. This was truly odd. We were 66 and 63, and did not appear feeble or unable to change a tire. In today's world, two people changing a tire in broad daylight, with backs to the highway so that a passerby could not determine our age or physical condition, certainly does not raise a red flag for a young man traveling in the opposite direction to turn around to help. When I explained that Jay had just gone through heart surgery and that I was very concerned, he replied: "I know, Jesus sent me." I was amazed and just knew that the Lord had heard my prayers. Despite Jay's reluctance to allow him to help, the young man told him in no uncertain terms to pay attention to his wife, get up, and allow him to take care of the problem. He plunged into the job immediately, working hard to unfasten the bolts that were extremely tight, constantly speaking of Jesus and how people should help each other. He even had a new hydraulic jack in his van which was still in its box, and got the tire changed swiftly. When the job was completed, I asked his name which was Larry, thanked him with all my heart and gave him a kiss. I asked if he had a card, and Larry handed us each a card which we put away as we said our goodbyes, leaving us with a tube of a special foam tire sealer. He rushed off, and when we looked at the cards he had given us, we could not believe our eyes. The cards read: "Jesus loves you so much, it hurts." They portrayed a bleeding hand pierced with a nail. We both still carry Larry's card in our wallets as proof of our angel encounter in the Everglades. I know that Larry was a special angel on earth that God had sent to save Jay from a crisis in a spot where help was not to be had. A few days later back home Adele brought me a small book identifying an angel encounter, and our encounter met all the features: the angel is not summoned; it comes of its own volition; the angel offers help and speaks of Jesus; the angel helps and quickly leaves. We will never forget Larry, our angel.

You can see that I have had clouds and some rain, but I have rapped and rapped and the Lord has delivered each time. Today, my past problems appear minor by comparison to real tragedies and to the many terrible adversities that are happening every day in other people's lives. I believe God strengthened my faith by testing me, and his mission for me is to reach others to find Him as I did. I believe that if my share of problems has been light, and they have all been overcome happily, it has been because God has been my ally and source of strength. I know that these beautiful outcomes that some people label "luck" and I call blessings have come about because I have learned to talk to God with absolute faith and have prayed passionately and persistently, trusting Him blindly. At each crossroad, with each challenge, He came to the rescue. Sometimes He gave me unquestionable and clear signs which I heeded, and, other times, it took longer but in the end His answer always appeared. I always know I am not talking to a vacuum but to Him who is listening. He listens to those who acknowledge his existence and power and believe in his compassion.

I am not alone in experiencing this absolute faith. I know others, who are as happy as I, and they too have found God in the same way and have received many blessings in answered prayers. They have good marriages, good children, good health, and a very happy outlook on life. They all agree that living with God and keeping Him close to their lives has been the power that has made them happy.

I know that problems have to exist, but we must face them with deep faith in God realizing we are not alone. If we acknowledge God and knock at His door, He is there and will always answer your call, but it is up to you to find the way to connect with true and absolute faith. Superficial prayers without really believing that we are talking to God are seldom heard. Going to church every Sunday and repeating prayers in robot-like fashion and singing church hymns alone will not do it. It has to be a very personal tete-a-tete with God with complete belief He is listening, opening your heart to Him with all your fears, concerns and anxieties. And, then watching for His signs. **Try it!**

CHAPTER 14

Woman And Man

In this earth of ours God has created two distinctly different beings: Woman and Man. Even the most avid feminist must admit the very simple but fundamental reality that it was intended that there should be two kinds—biologically and physically different— or we would have been created all men or all women. Two kinds, not one superior to the other, but one just as essential and important as the other, one as much in need of the other, complementing each other, but definitely different in many ways. We must acknowledge this basic truth despite what the Women's Lib movement might advocate, and celebrate the importance of Woman and Man. The feminists would have you believe that woman and man are equal—sexually, intellectually, even physically—- but the fact remains we are not, our hormones make us different, and this difference is beautiful, attractive, and should not be destroyed because it does not undermine one kind or the other.

I will not attempt to explain homosexuality as there are many theories as to why this deviation in sex exists. I just wish it would not have occurred thereby creating a difference in sexual orientation outside the original intent to procreate. Statistically, this change has affected only a small number, approximately 2%, of the population in our country. As a Christian I believe in showing love and kindness to everyone, and I do not condone discrimination of homosexuals. They should not be shunned, ridiculed or mocked or be treated unfairly. I respect their dignity as I do that of all human beings. I have homosexual friends, and in fact, one of my best friends as a teenager was a homosexual whom I loved dearly. But, I resent that the homosexuality issue be used as a political movement to gain votes or to create class strife. Unfortunately, although a minority, some homosexuals have been misled by this movement, to show contempt and disrespect for heterosexuals, in an arrogant manner. In so doing, they appear to be making a statement that homosexuality is a superior manifestation of sex. Just as I find sad and unjust that they be treated unfairly, I do not approve of their being used as a political tool. Sexual difference is a social issue which needs to be addressed with love, education, and acceptance.

In this chapter, I focus on the natural and beautiful difference that exists in the majority of women and men.

Woman has been challenged to be mother, lover, homemaker, and companion, yet still reserve her individuality as a person in pursuing personal interests, sometimes outside the home and family. Experience has proven woman is capable of playing all these roles well, and in so doing, find the fulfillment she is seeking. No woman should have doubts on the joy of being a woman or should feel she must find herself through a liberation movement or be compelled to defy Man to establish her identity and God-given importance.

Man should not need to castrate his masculinity in order to show gentleness and sensitivity or to be capable of performing duties heretofore considered only for women. We must explore our potential and remain true to who we are because it is this difference between Woman and Man that makes us attractive to each other. There is no need to stamp out differences between Woman and Man, but rather we should develop our inherent powers to their fullest capacity and learn to be happy, accepting our differences and proudly playing our important roles in life as Woman and Man.

In our country today women have attained a most enviable position, enjoying all of the legal rights and other privileges of men, but in many cases, avoiding some of men's responsibilities, hiding behind their femininity. Through the years, women have been emancipated from the unfair social prejudices and legal injustices that existed, and today's woman is a liberated individual with the intelligence and aggressiveness to be economically self-sufficient. She can drive, handle the budget, pursue the career of her choice in whatever field, and do practically anything she feels capable of handling without being censored, curtailed, or discriminated in any way because of sex.

In my opinion, women have reached a summit that offers them all the opportunities they could desire without taking away from them the special treatment which men naturally wish to bestow on them. In other words, they have the best of two worlds. My fear is that in further pursuing the liberation quest, some women are losing their precious femininity that is so attractive to men. It is the quality in women that inspires most men to be their champions and to want to do for them those beautiful things most women enjoy. Some women have become so forceful in dealing with men that men regard them as another man and competitor. Essentially, these women, knowingly or not, are wiping out the natural difference that exists between woman and man.

I believe that women should realize they need not strive any longer as a movement, but enjoy the special status that is Woman's alone: capable enough to attempt all that man can, but feminine enough not to be allowed by him to attempt those things he wants to do for her, his attractive and softer companion. While socially and in every other way, women can enjoy the same rights and privileges that men have, most women are grateful they do not have to worry about assuming truly masculine responsibilities, as long as there are men who can assume them for her.

Women today in our country are very capable of representing a strong force to be contended with if they had to fight to preclude injustices and sex discrimination from recurring in any area where equal rights are justified. They should not fear losing the gains obtained as this fear would reflect an underestimation of women's intelligence and power.

Women are still challenged in the area of equal pay versus men. I believe that women in public service have the power and ability to strive for a law that will give them this equality with men provided a woman has equal or superior qualifications than her male counterpart. Toward this end, perhaps efforts on women's behalf should be pursued in government just as any other civil right. It is my opinion, however, that whatever inequality in pay that may exist in the private sector should be corrected without legal intervention. The challenge is in the hands of women themselves who can aggressively and boldly demonstrate their competence and capability to perform their responsibilities with the same or greater excellence than that of men at the same job. When this level of equal or greater competence exists, a woman can demand this recognition in the private sector. However, I believe that the issue of pay inequality should not be based simply on the grounds of being a woman but earned by merit. In the same manner that men in seeking better pay have to show superior performance, so should women.

When a woman marries or has a mate, it is comforting to know that although she has the option to work outside the home because it offers her fulfillment or because she wishes to help with the finances, she also has the option to stay home. This latter option remains open to women and can be chosen at any time during the relationship that she prefers to stay home and adapt to her man's income. I do not believe there would be many men who would not graciously accede to a woman's decision to revert to the traditional position of housewife. In contrast, I do not know of any healthy, capable and well balanced man who would prefer to stop working for no justifiable reason other than to stay home and adapt to his wife's income. Perhaps, such isolated cases may exist, but if a man chooses such an option, I believe it would reflect poorly on his masculinity. I don't think that a woman would be too keen to accept such a proposition from a healthy capable man.

The double-privilege status that many women enjoy is clearly demonstrated with women married to wealthy affluent men. These women not only exercise the option of staying home, but also enjoy a true life of leisure with outside help that allows them to do little in the home. In the meantime, their men keep working and producing for them. In my book, today it is definitely a woman's world.

If women are clever enough to recognize the beauty of their special status, they would stop pushing further and just enjoy these wonderful double privileges now available to them. Most women that retain their femininity will never have to change a tire, unless it is her choice, or have to catch an ugly frog or roach, unless she is one of the more courageous ones who can handle these creatures. I think most women would much prefer cooking or decorating to heavy yard work, fixing the sprinkler system, or checking what is wrong with the car.

Of course, we know there are some women who are very handy and mechanical and can do most of the jobs that have customarily been considered masculine. We are also aware there are some men who are not handy at fixing things, lack mechanical aptitude, and cannot even change a bulb or perform any of the chores traditionally regarded as men's. Consequently today both men and women should do that for which they have more aptitude, regardless of sex. Nonetheless, it is rewarding to know that even when the woman can better handle the house painting job, if she remains true to her kind and keep her feminine touch, her man will want to move heavy objects for her, assist her anytime his normally greater strength can be put at her service, and always be there to protect and defend her. Most men instinctively like to do for women, theirs and others, if allowed to display their natural desire to be protective and to utilize their greater strength in behalf of women. Whenever a man does not feel this way about a woman, it is usually because that woman's behavior has provoked in him this apathy towards her. She has either tried to outdo him or has demanded his help in a domineering authoritative way instead of using her irresistible God-given femininity.

There are no traditional roles any longer, and each mate should help the other in every way that is necessary and fair, but this equitable arrangement does not change the fact that most women in a relationship enjoy catering to their men, cooking for them, keeping their house, and raising their children or that most men, despite the fact that they can do the dishes and take care of the children, still enjoy being women's strong man and protector. Most women rely on their men when they hear strange noises in the middle of the night, and the dog won't stop barking. They quietly tap their men in fear, and it is very reassuring to know that he will get up to check. Men instinctively would not allow their women to venture into any possible danger. Most women appreciate and enjoy having this kind of a protective partner, and most men want to be this kind of partner for their women. It is up to women to not ruin the well-balanced partnership that has developed now that past injustices and unfairness have been corrected.

I am aware that many of the statements in this chapter could be considered to apply more to the man/woman relationship. However, many also apply to all women and all men, whether with mate or single, because femininity and masculinity, under the original intent of two distinct sexes, should always be retained. All women should inspire in men their manly instinct to be gallant, protective, and courteous, and similarly, all men should command respect from women as well as be respectful, and always be ready to help any woman in distress.

Women need to maintain the beautiful difference that exists between them and men. I am certain there are many women who share my feelings. It is a shame that a relatively small group of dissatisfied and discontent women, often with a political agenda, make content women appear to men as the women they are not.

Even in today's modern society, when we compare man and woman, generally speaking and we all know there are exceptions, we find most men are stronger physically, desire to be providers for their family, are less afraid of physical peril than women, are ready to sacrifice and defend their families at all cost, wish to be gallant with all women, offer women their seats, wish to carry things for them, and can solve more mechanical problems than women. We should recognize these truths and compliment and appreciate Man for playing the role for which God has equipped him rather than trying to take away from his masculinity in a competitive fashion.

On the other hand, we find that most women, with or without careers, single or not, enjoy cooking, decorating, fashion and attractive clothes, have an innate maternal and nurturing instinct, and are blessed with a natural intangible and abstract quality that is present wherever she is. She fills her home, her office or place of work or business, with a special warmth that seems to be missing in a place that is womanless. We should celebrate the beautiful contrast between Woman and Man.

I am a very typical woman. I am feminine and proud of it. I boast of being a woman and would not want to be anything else. Similarly, my husband is a typical man—masculine and proud of it. He would not want to be anything else. I do not feel inferior to any man. I know I can do anything a man can do intellectually and in many other ways. I certainly know myself as not lacking in aggressiveness and drive, whenever it is needed or required of me. Since I am not good at manual or mechanical abilities, I cede to most in this department, but without contempt or hang-ups. In fact, I cede to women as well who are better than I in these areas. I am liberated enough to repudiate male injustices, but I know I could not fall victim to the so-called "male chauvinist" or abusive type. They can only thrive with women who lack self-esteem and who have not learned to love themselves first without feelings of guilt. These women would probably be victims to other women as well.

I like and admire men and do not consider them my enemy or competitor, but regard them as a companion on whom I can rely. I do not hesitate to tell them how great "it is to have a man around the house." As a result, men have always liked to do things for me spontaneously and gallantly, and frankly, I love it! I am happy to do for them also spontaneously everything I can that comes natural to me with that special womanly way we alone possess. Many a time I have found my car would not start or that one of my tires was hideously flat or that I had left my key locked in the car. I always had more than one man come to my rescue to give me a hand because I just act like and am the kind of woman a man would not leave stranded.

Similarly, as this kind of woman, I like my role as a woman of being a hostess and of creating a pleasant atmosphere for men. When my husband is outside working in the yard or doing any other kind of physical work, he need not ask me for a cold drink because I will always anticipate his needs. And, when I serve his meal, I think of everything he would want and present dinner to him in the most attractive of ways so that he will feel like a king. I am happy to do for him just as he always does for me.

When we went sailing years ago sometimes I was placed in the predicament of being First Mate when there was just the two of us. I was eternally grateful when we had a man aboard that relieved me of the very unpleasant duties that are far from natural or easy for me. Try as I did, and believe me, I really did try to be helpful, I realized I did not have a natural knack for tying knots, keeping the boat on course or knowing which way the wind was blowing. I just did not have the physical strength needed for some boating chores. But, I tried to fill in for these inabilities by enthusiastically doing those I could. I supplied nice music on the radio, quenched Jay's thirst with cold water or beer, prepared a nice lunch, and never forgot the munchies he enjoyed. The best First Mate in the world could not surpass my ability to keep a happy and enthusiastic mood prevailing to add to his sailing relaxation. Those are my feminine abilities that come natural to me, and I was quick to offer them just as I could count on my Capitan to keep that boat sailing on course for me.

Watching Jay rigging the boat, lifting the mast, fixing that dreadful emergency motor that seemed to conk out when we needed it most going under a bridge or pulling into dock, throwing that anchor over and over again because sometimes it just would not catch, and generally facing all the numerous difficulties that can arise in sailing, as a woman I felt great admiration for his obvious masculinity. I do not speak for any other woman, but I know I could not have a sailboat if a man did not come with it because there is no way I would know what to do when that motor refuses to start and has to be taken apart and the spark plugs cleaned and all kinds of odd things happen of which I do not have the slightest notion. Let alone these purely mechanical requirements, how could I ever get that 25-foot 75-lb. mast up by myself like Jay was capable of doing. During the years we sailed I met many other first-mate wives and girlfriends in our sailing club that experienced similar sailing inadequacies and shared much of my same feelings about sailing without a man.

Many women would like to be selective in their liberation approach. They would like to believe they are man's equal in every respect and to compete with man, but as soon as they are in a real bind they can't handle, they revert to being a woman. Sometimes it just takes a cute frog waiting to jump at her or a bug for her to scream for a man's help and to forget all about woman-man equality.

Some women exercise their option to stay at home and take care of their small children, and although they will be very busy at times, they might also be able to sleep late many mornings while their mates are up very early for work. These women enjoy a life where many of their demands, deadlines and priorities are self-imposed, set and controlled by them, in contrast to those to which their mates must adhere with the structured schedule and demands their jobs require. While their mates are busy at work, they may be able to enjoy a soap opera and flexible breaks. I do not believe these women ever questioned their right to take up this option nor did they ever ask their mates if they preferred to switch roles. This type of woman enjoys the benefits that accrue to her just for being a woman but is quick to claim her liberation from men without realizing she is enjoying a privileged position just because she is a woman. There are many such women, and I am not criticizing them for enjoying the privileges, but for not admitting and accepting that they are different from Man and for so unfairly defying Man as an enemy instead of a partner.

In the drive to wipe out all differences between Man and Woman to a degree that is neither natural nor beneficial to Woman, some women have been successful in destroying masculinity in their men, which I find rather upsetting. Just as femininity is one of woman's most appealing qualities to men so is masculinity to women. Masculinity, like femininity, is a quality on which we cannot quite place our finger, but it can be sensed very keenly. It reflects physical capability and strength, courage and guts, ruddiness coupled with gentleness towards Woman. It is probably the quality women most respect and admire in men in the same way that men love woman's femininity. Yet, some women in trying to become just like Man in every respect, challenging Man like another Man, have managed to intimidate some weaker men into losing the one quality that so distinguishes them in the eyes of Woman. Many men today react and respond to the strong masculine-type female with such lack of masculinity that these women have lost all respect for them. Actually, manly women really would prefer stronger men who would stand up to them when they are acting unfairly or going too far, rather than having men become victims to their domineering approach. Ironically, in their aggressive battle for more and more, these women have destroyed in some men the one trait they probably subconsciously want most in them.

As you seek happiness which is the ultimate goal, I want to again stress my message to both women and men:

Women, please keep in mind that regardless of how modern and liberated you may be, you should keep one of your most valuable and desirable assets: femininity. You should be happy you are a woman and hold on to this amazing trait that is yours and that makes you a wife, a mate, a lover, a mother, and a woman itself. Once you have convinced yourself of your importance as a woman, have recognized what a wonderful and unique position you have with the best of two worlds available to you, you can begin to enjoy the great life that can be yours and stop competing with men. You need to concentrate instead on yourself and on how you can improve yourself into a happier life.

Men, my message to you in your search for happiness is to not allow disrespect from women who have reversed their role. You should demand to be treated with the same dignity that women demand, and to retain your masculinity because it is the trait that makes you attractive to women. You must insist on keeping the liberation pendulum in balance. You should win women's respect by being everything a man should be: strong, protective, supportive but also tender, sensitive, courteous and gallant. You should always show respect for women but also demand respect from women. You should not allow woman to attempt against your masculinity because in the end she will like and respect you less for it. You were placed in this world for the purpose of being woman's partner, lover, companion and protector and as a man to be different from woman. You should not try to imitate her but complement her and never allow a woman to destroy the masculine quality in you that separates you from her.

Viva la difference!

CHAPTER 15

A Happy And Lasting Marriage: Our Most Exciting And Difficult Challenge

Deep true love between a man and woman is beautiful, whether in marriage or not. I am not referring to meaningless man/woman relations with little or no personal involvement in which sex alone plays the dominant part over everything else, but of that sublime unique feeling a man and woman experience when their entire existences merge into one, physically and spiritually, and life becomes impossible one without the other. I realize there are unmarried couples who have this very meaningful relationship; however, I have found that those I have known in unmarried relationships would much have preferred to be married to their lovers, if the decision were theirs alone to make, but circumstances of one kind or another interfered with reaching this goal. I do not mean to say that one should wish to marry just for the sake of being married. However, it is a fact that most men and women do wish to marry if they find the right soul-mate for whom they have developed feelings of true love, admiration, and respect.

There is no reason why we should deny this normal healthy desire for fear of being considered old-fashioned and out of time. Most happy persons wish to find true and lasting love and to become united in a permanent way with their lovers in marriage. Oftentimes, we hear single men and women boasting about their free independent lives, but I have yet to meet any who would not alter their single status if the right person came into their lives. If such persons do exist who honestly feel completely fulfilled and sincerely happy without the remotest desire to become united in marriage to a person they could love and respect, I apologize for generalizing and urge them to continue this pursuit of happiness that evidently works for them.

But, if you are, like most of us, desirous to love, to be loved, and to belong to one person, and wish to be fulfilled as a lover and husband or wife, as you have every right to be, then you will see in marriage your most exciting challenge. I have found such fulfillment and happiness in my marriage that I can truly say that after all these years if I were given a second chance, I would marry the same man all over again.

Decidedly, marriage must have deep roots in most of us when both men and women who free themselves of the legal union through divorce or whose partner has passed, generally try again within a short time after. It would seem that if marriage were such an unnatural relationship, as we are sometimes led to believe in these modern times, those who had experienced failure in marriage would be very reluctant to find themselves again trapped in this binding union. Yet, we all know this is not so. Men, who traditionally have sought and defended their freedom more than women are no exception to this natural desire to try again at marriage after a marital failure. Because of all of this and my own personal experience, I am an ardent believer in marriage as the ideal union between a man and a woman in love. Logically, my approach to the man/woman relationship is taken first as a wife, but the ingredients I have pointed out in this chapter that are needed for a happy marriage apply to both husband and wife.

A wife or husband is a combination of lover, friend, and companion and consequently, the person who can best complement and meet the multiple needs of the other partner. In spite of the innate differences between woman and man, both play a most important role in a happy marriage.

Their individual roles converge in meeting these three important objectives:

First, both husband and wife will fulfill their own basic desire to love and be loved. The husband will be committed to protect and support his wife in every way. The wife will satisfy her desire to be needed by this man, to belong to him, and to care for him. Together they will create a family.

Second, if they are successful in keeping the marriage alive and making the relationship everything it should be, they will have created happiness not only for themselves but also for their children. Good parents of necessity must be successful wives and husbands. It is only through keeping this relationship genuinely happy and stable that they will be able to give their children the healthy atmosphere of love, happiness and security they need so much to develop into happy adults. We know that divorces are damaging not only to the partners but to the children as well who suffer greatly with the separation of their two most important role models. Children from broken homes already begin the game of life with a handicap. An intelligent mother knows that she must keep Daddy happy, and she must not neglect him because of excessive dedication to the children which some women tend to do. Children who are shown they are loved and admired in the million ways parents are capable accept that Mom has to take care and love Dad also. An intelligent father knows that he will earn his children's respect by showing love, respect and support for his wife in every way and that he will instill these values in the children which they will imitate in their later lives.

And, **finally**, by creating a happy marriage for themselves and their children, they will be happy individually also and will be better equipped to face their responsibilities with optimism and enthusiasm. Their home will be their paradise, and both husband and wife will be the King and Queen of the den.

Of all our relationships, none is probably more complex and difficult than marriage, but this fact also makes the challenge of creating a happy lasting marriage tremendously exciting. To unite and keep in marital bliss two persons of diverse backgrounds in most cases, with different personality traits, emotional makeup, and interests and aspirations, is not something that can be accomplished by mere love, sexual magic or just luck. A good marriage can only be achieved by continuously working at the business of getting along which requires, besides love, much compromise, intelligence, respect and understanding of human behavior. A man and woman must continue working at the relationship and growing as individuals as long as they remain married, if the marriage is to remain vibrant and happy.

All of the principles outlined in this book to guarantee a happy life as an individual certainly apply to marriage since a happy person forcibly makes a better partner than an unhappy one, but marriage requires much more.

The following recommendations apply to both husbands and wives:

Fundamentally, marriage needs to be nurtured with much love and affection— the kind of love that is allowed to flow freely and is shown in every way, with words and actions. Of what value is love that is perhaps felt deeply but not shown, and only exists in the heart and mind of the person who loves? Men need to be shown love just as much women. Wives must actively show their love to their husbands, and they will reap the results by receiving greater love from their husbands in return.

I learned through hard experience that just loving, without showing it, is not enough for a man. I was unable to express my love freely to my husband. I knew I loved him, and I thought I was showing it to him in many subtle ways, until one day, after a series of deep discussions and many years of marriage, he confessed how much he had been missing my active demonstrations of affection. I had never seen myself as unaffectionate and did not realize my husband had kept track of many seemingly small ways of expressing and showing love. The incident triggered in me the desire to overcome this inability to be openly affectionate with my husband. I believe I had some type of mental block that prevented me from coming out with all of the love I felt for him.

I forced myself to change because I recognized he had given me a signal, and I was not about to allow a hang-up to dampen the wonderful relationship we had. I began slowly to penetrate the mental barrier that hampered my love-showing abilities until I liberated myself from the terrible inhibition which I had accepted as a natural trait in women. I grew up erroneously believing that it was the man who had to show love more aggressively. It was not easy, and at times, coming out strong with affection was very unnatural to me. Changing long-established behavior patterns never is easy, but quite possible if you are willing to change and imperative when the behavior pattern is damaging to your happiness. I am now fully capable of actively showing love to my husband in many ways, some passive, some exciting, but this new ability seems to grow from day to day, and there is renewed vitality in our marriage because of this change in me. In return, my husband also is more affectionate.

Once the basic love-showing need is satisfied, perhaps the next most important ingredient in a marriage is good communication. Men tend to communicate less than women, and the intelligent wife must encourage communication since we are conditioned ever since we were little girls to say whatever was bothering or worrying us, with less pride intervention than our partners. It is much harder for most men to communicate, but we must patiently extract the pieces of precious information, bit by bit, and keep the lines always open. We must not allow silence to substitute what should be said in the belief that the problem will go away if ignored or not discussed. Quite to the contrary, the problem does not go away, but lingers on as a skeleton in the closet waiting to come out in some other form and shape to haunt the relationship. It is much better to air a problem entirely, with respect and without resorting to harsh injurious insults. This can be done.

In my years of marriage, I have always put this principle into practice, and after much tactful information extraction, my husband does communicate more, although never quite as much as I. Heated arguments can be very damaging since much of what is said, under the influence of anger, can be extremely hurtful and not easily forgotten after the wave of anger wave has passed. Hurtful words and actions may appear forgotten, but many times, they can be lurking unnoticed and be the underlying cause of a later negative reaction which cannot be readily associated with the insults exchanged quite some time before.

Objective discussions with free communication and exposure of thoughts are necessary and healthy to a marriage. It is naïve to believe that such a complex and intimate relationship can exist in complete harmony without the need to discuss openly differences and problems. This must be done within a framework of respect, and each partner must understand the other's viewpoint by listening to the other side of the issue. Listening will give an insight as to the why of our partner's actions and will help settle the problem amicably so that both can return as quickly as possible to the more rewarding aspect of marriage of tender loving and happy living together.

In the years we have lived together I have never let my husband fall asleep with an unresolved problem. I have used our many womanly devices to return the relationship to cordiality before the beginning of a new day. With intelligence, women have the ability to continue the discussion until it is resolved and not allow it to carry over to the next day. Humor, apology, show of affection, flirtation, sex, and probably many more tactics can be employed. All are good and should be used to conclude an argument so that tomorrow the problem will not be facing the couple.

Now that we have a marriage that is bursting with love that is actively expressed with words and deeds, and not taken for granted, and that we are communicating and discussing our problems with respect, I suggest some important pointers I have learned through the years that have contributed to our happy union.

- **<u>Let your partner be an individual.</u>**

    Many partners have a natural desire to control their spouse's life from the moment the marriage contract is signed. You should realize that you are husband and wife and not mother and father with control over your small children. The spouse is merely a man or woman who has become an intimate part of the other's life with the purpose of creating happiness for each other in the union without infringing on the personal freedom or individuality of the other. If you realize this fact, you will be happier and hence more capable of making your partner happy. If freedom of action prevails in those interests the spouse wishes to pursue, you will have taken one major step forward. Each partner is an individual, and both must be able to grow individually in those areas in which they need fulfillment. The partners must find this needed freedom and expansion in the marriage so that neither feels trapped. The reward will be a happier marriage. A spouse that feels free as an individual will always prefer to be with the partner. If all the right ingredients are there, no spouse will lose the other simply because of freedom to be an individual.

- **<u>Keep sex alive and well.</u>**

Marriage cannot keep its vitality on a purely spiritual or platonic basis. Sex plays an extremely important part in this intimate relationship which in all probability began and was spurred to consummation precisely by physical attraction. Both husband and wife have to keep sex in the marriage alive and well. Any sexual inhibitions you may have brought into the marriage from your childhood must be overcome, and you need to understand that between a man and a woman in marriage nothing is taboo. You must also recognize that sex is a beautiful expression of love between a husband and wife.

- **Admire your partner.**

  Admiration, like love, needs to be expressed. Admiration is a key ingredient for a happy marriage. Sometimes men try to feign a need for praise, but they need to be admired just as much as women. We all need words of praise and encouragement. You must profess faith in each other. Women have always thrived on compliments from their husbands, but men similarly need to be told they are strong, attractive, and intelligent. You must not squander on admiration. It nurtures the marriage.

- **Earn your partner's admiration.**

  Love and attraction are not static sentiments. They can be kindled to great heights or they can be allowed to die gradually. When we think of sex inevitably we think of physical attraction. However, the fact that we are living in a world with an overabundance of women poses a more potential competitive problem for wives. For this reason, I emphasize that wives do everything possible to keep attractive and appealing to their husbands, regardless of age. This can be done by doing what is needed to keep in good health, to control weight, to have good grooming and cleanliness habits, and to dress in good taste.

Partners must also grow intellectually so that interesting conversation can exist between them. You must be able to discuss work and current matters of interest to both. There are many other areas in which you can win your partner's admiration besides physical or intellectual. A husband's ability for house repair work makes him appear resourceful to his wife, and a woman's culinary abilities as well as her hostess charm can earn words of admiration from her husband. Her husband will admire her creative talents or good taste in decorating the home of which he is so proud. You should strive to make yourselves worthy of your partner's admiration, physically and otherwise. I have noticed that when spouses show admiration for each other in various ways, invariably this is a clear indicator that they have kept the spark of love very much alive. The show of mutual admiration is excellent proof that the partners are actively in love.

- **<u>Be an interesting companion.</u>**
No marriage can survive happily when a man and woman cannot enjoy time together alone. This is definitely a test of a happy marriage. The man and woman

who can enjoy each other's company and can have conversation as they did during the courting days can safely conclude they have a good thing going. This quality in a marriage must be cultivated so that when faced in a setting of the two alone, they will not see each other as strangers with no common interests and with nothing to talk about. After all is said and done, and the initial years of passionate fury give way to other stages or phases of love in the marriage, it is quite sad to see a man and woman, united in marriage, who cannot enjoy conversation and companionship and who are not stimulated with each other's presence.

- **<u>Do not sit on your laurels.</u>**

You must be alert to changing needs as the marriage grows. A happy marriage does not just happen—-it is created. There is much work, much compromise, and much love that goes into it. A happy marriage is not achieved at a given time and expected to remain permanently happy unless the man and woman continue growing and working at the relationship. Each stage of marriage poses different problems and challenges that threaten the relationship at that particular stage, regardless of the happiness achieved in a previous one. And, again the partners must confront the new problems and cope with them to win yet another victory for the marriage and give it further solidarity.

A wife is faced with probably one of the most serious challenges in the marriage if her man falls prey to the much talked-about psychological male menopause through which many men go after 40. This can be a very taxing time for the marriage with several challenges converging. At that particular time in the marriage the children are probably in their teens and also going through a difficult stage. The couple probably has been married more than 20 years. Consequently, the marriage will be facing pressure from two fronts. Matters can be aggravated if the marriage has lost some luster because of past errors committed in their relationship. Unfortunately, it is the wife who will have to carry the brunt of the burden during this crisis. At this very crucial time, a wife's understanding of what is occurring to her heretofore wonderful husband can be very valuable. If she lacks the knowledge and understanding of what her husband is experiencing psychologically, she might judge his actions as unfair and offensive and respond defensively further alienating the husband precisely at a time when he needs much more love and attention.

She may also open herself to the vulnerability that another woman might offer him the love and attention he is missing. Instead, through patience, love, and understanding, the wife can help her husband weather this tremendous conflict and emotional turmoil. She should search her own soul for areas in which she might have failed and try to improve her attitudes and style of interaction in an effort to make their lives together happier and more interesting. She now needs to inject new stimulants into the marriage, using her creativity and imagination to eliminate routine and lack of excitement. She should plan to get away just the two to some spot where they can rediscover each other without the pressures and problems of everyday living. An unexpected sexy nightgown will certainly arouse a husband at any age, but in the autumn years it can do wonders.

The wife should become interested and participate in activities the husband has been doing alone, such as bowling, boating, fishing, or golfing, which will make her a more enjoyable companion. Anything that can add variety to the marriage and give the partners an opportunity to enjoy each other in a fresher, different and more exciting way will do the relationship much good during this delicate stage of marriage.

Whatever the challenge, you can be certain the job is never fully done, and you cannot sit back and completely relax based on your past victories. That is why marriage is so exciting!

- **Watch out for the million "little things" that can make or break a marriage.**
In such an intimate and complex relationship, where two distinctly different people with diverse likes and dislikes, interests and personality, vow to unite for life

and attempt to live happily and in peace ever after, there are millions of small things that can cause a marriage to breakdown—much more than one single big problem. Conversely, there are also many small goodwill-creating actions that can strengthen the marriage.

Partners should thank each other whenever the other does something helpful. It does not have to be something major. A thank you is always well received when the husband performs any task in the house even if it could be considered part of his obligations. Similarly, a thank you is much appreciated by a wife when she irons her husband's shirt or does any other favor for her husband. There are many ways for a couple to create good and positive feelings in the marriage. An unexpected phone call at the office just to remind a husband or wife how much he or she is loved can create an enormous amount of good vibes for the marriage. An affectionate card or personal note expressing your feelings of love slipped unexpectedly under the bathroom door or on the pillow will cause a wonderful spark in the marriage and add to the love reservoir. A gentleman husband that opens the car door for his wife wins many points in her heart's scoreboard. A considerate wife caring for a tired husband, an attentive husband that serves his wife breakfast in bed and a wife that surprises her husband with his favorite meal are all ways of growing love in small ways that help the marriage endure happily. Logically, if you have more positive actions and less negative ones, you have better chances of creating a good marriage.

Couples many times forget the many small offenses of which they have been guilty. They do not realize that these little jabs build up and remain consciously or subconsciously alive in the mind of the offended partner, causing hidden resentment that can gradually destroy all the love that existed at the onset of the marriage. Sometimes we hear of divorces in which neither or both of the partners can understand what happened that made the marriage disintegrate. No one major problem could be signaled out as the cause. Infidelity wasn't a factor—neither partner was interested in anyone else. No big in-law problems or financial difficulties existed. Neither had a drinking problem and basically both were good people who had entered the marriage with love and an honest desire to make it last. Yet, the marriage had gradually fallen apart, and there was no more love left in one or both of the partners. Neither could explain exactly how this had happened in terms of one major single cause. They just could not stand each other; living together was not fun anymore, and it was impossible to stay together any longer.

If these couples could have listened to a playback or watched a replay of their lives together during the years, they would have been astonished at the million little things that had gone wrong, that had caused much bitterness and resentment, and had finally destroyed their love. Now, neither partner could trace their marriage failure to the many times when one had hurt the other's pride and ego with blunt criticism.

So many negative actions had been forgotten. They did not remember cutting-down remarks. The wife could not recall when she had stopped waiting to have dinner with her husband and left him to have dinner alone night after night or when she had hurt him deeply rejecting his family, but always imposing her own. She had long forgotten the many times she had made her husband lose authority with the children by disagreeing with his decisions in front of them. The husband could not remember the many times he had not complimented his wife when she wore a new dress or got a new hairdo. Forgotten too were the many times the husband would come to an empty house, disorganized and messy, to find no dinner. They had long since stopped doing things together, and each went his or her own way. Out of memory also were the times when he wanted to bring a guest for dinner that was important to him, and she complained so bitterly that he finally desisted. The husband could not recall those times that his wife was overworked, and he sat idly in the couch. The wife could not remember those times when he wanted so much to go fishing or golfing with the guys or to watch a game, and he had to break his plans because she had gotten so upset. There was that ugly but comfortable chair he so much enjoyed, but that absolutely ruined the decor, so it had to go.

Forgotten also were those times when one or the other, in a thrust of anger had hit below the belt, attacking the partner in areas of great vulnerability to the ego as only a husband or wife is capable of doing because of their intimate knowledge of one another.

We all have known women who keep such a beautiful and immaculate home that their husbands feel like company in their own house so that they prefer spending time elsewhere where they can relax, prop up their feet on the table, and spread their newspapers on the floor. We also know of men and women who are hypochondriacs, perpetually complaining of imaginary illnesses. They are always tired and not enthusiastic about doing anything or going anywhere. And there are the domineering outspoken women who treat their husbands rudely especially in front of others.

Put together all of these and many other similar and seemingly small things, during a prolonged period, and you have the reason for the breakdown. If the husband or wife had found someone appealing who did not make the husband feel stupid or who made the wife feel beautiful, someone who didn't complain or offer injurious or sarcastic remarks, that someone would be blamed for the divorce, when actually that someone was merely a by-product of the forgotten million small underlying causes that destroy love and ultimately a marriage.

There are so many small things that do not fall into any one big category that it is difficult to list them all. But these million small injuries which should be avoided could be eliminated almost entirely if husbands and wives would apply:

The Golden Rule
Common sense
Intelligence
Tact
Love with minimal possessiveness and
All the highlighted pointers outlined in this chapter and just never, never stop working at it.

Perhaps, this task might seem next to impossible, but as difficult and demanding as it may be the reward of succeeding at life's most exciting and difficult challenge is immense. You will have created a happy and lasting marriage that will offer you in return all the love you desire as well as provide your children with the family stability they need to bloom into happy adults. Some task, some reward!

CHAPTER 16

People Molding–Our Most Creative Role

When I think of the various roles for which we were intended, I must start with the one which above all others, is the most creative, affects humanity more significantly, and has more transcendental consequences: parenthood. Parents are the true molders of humankind. No one can command or wield more power than parents. When we were endowed with this sublime opportunity, we were chosen to be the most important persons in another person's formative life. Nothing can parallel this relationship. Only parents can create or destroy, influence, and cause life-lasting effects on a person during early childhood. With such unique molding powers, we have in our hands the possibility of making or breaking our children during their early years. Every person, regardless of adult importance and achievements, was influenced as a child and molded by that most important Mother and Father. Only parents possess this special God-bestowed gift.

We have established that each person comes into this world with certain innate traits, and that this is the fabric with which parents must weave to produce a happy adult. We also know that these traits can be desirable, making the job easier, but many times they are less than desirable making the parenting task much more difficult. Regardless of this fact, we must enter parenthood with the awareness and complete conviction that our role is important and crucial. We cannot take lightly the responsibility we assumed when we became parents because as people-molders we directly affect the lives of our children in a positive or negative way.

We must recognize that parents are only imperfect human beings, not magicians, but this reality should not give us license for poor parenting because the results can be devastating. When we perform this role with the knowledge that we are contributing to the creation of a well balanced adult, we have the power through love and intelligence to enhance the inherent traits of our child. Perhaps, we may not be entirely successful in some cases, but parents will achieve much in most cases by being the very best they can be.

We all need good parenting, and if we do not receive it, the child in us is greatly affected. When we are little, we are insecure and dependent, needing desperately the comfort and love of those all-important persons in our lives: Mom and Dad. They alone can make us feel better and reassure us that they will always be there unconditionally to help us. The unhappy child in us will inevitably affect the adult part of us in many negative ways and can create great unhappiness for us. Just to list a few: not reaching out and making friends, lack of self-esteem, a poor image of our appearance, etc. Psychiatrists explain that all of these feelings are an indication that the unhappy child is overrunning the adult part of us. So you can see how much misery can be wrought by parents who perform poorly.

Few of us assume the parenting role with all the preparation, knowledge, love, and dedication required. We are given the chance to take a baby and through love and care create a happy stable person who, in turn, will take his or her place in the world productively, and through a series of chain reactions, make our greatest contribution to humankind. Yet, many times we blow it!

Often we are searching for distant sources of fulfillment, and right at our hands, those of us blessed with being parents have the most creative challenge we will ever meet in our lifetime. Why is it we do not prepare more adequately to play this important role for which we were chosen and which by far can have such an impact on the world as a whole? I believe the reason why many fail as parents is primarily because of lack of understanding of the irreparable damage they can cause their children. We try to be good parents instinctively and feel that our errors can later be corrected so we go about the project of being parents with only superficial knowledge and interest. Oftentimes, because of this lack of knowledge, some totally destroy a child who otherwise would have developed into a happy adult.

Another reason why this important task of people-molding is so poorly handled and not performed with the excellence required is that possibly their parents before them also failed at their task, hence creating unhappy adults who are incapable of being good parents. There may be many other reasons for poor parenting, but we do know many parents are failing at this all-important job, and there is innumerable evidence in our society that confirms this. Psychiatrist offices are packed with unstable, unhappy, maladjusted people, with bags full of complexes, who did not receive the love they yearned for when they were babies. They had to learn the hard way to cope with life through self therapy or long drawn-out treatments. Many simply remain unhappy beings. In turn, these unhappy people create more unhappiness for others. Practically all of the maladies that plague our world today in one form or another stem from confused, sick people who to a great extent are the product of poor parenting. Many of these people could have been normal happy persons if the key figures in their formative years had played their part conscientiously.

We need to think about this human tragedy. In many cases, none of this misery need have happened if parents had done their job. This is why it is so vital that both women and men assume this most creative role with total devotion, unselfishness, and the knowledge that they are creating happiness and ultimately contributing to a better world.

How can we claim success in whatever field, regardless of our intellectual or material achievements, if we are not successful as parents in creating a happy person with high self-esteem? This should be the first item on any woman's or man's agenda when they decide to become a parent. All our other roles, important as they may be in their own right, must bow to that of being good parents. Nothing, absolutely nothing, can compare with the exceptional opportunity given to us to create a happy person through love, discipline and understanding.

However, if we were not able to accomplish this goal fully because of the child's innate undesirable personality traits, we should be totally certain that we selflessly offered all that we could to the child, especially love and a framework of respect and discipline. I believe that if we did our best, even when we may have had the misfortune of a naturally difficult child, we can feel successful in achieving a foundation for the child's happiness in its later years. With this foundation this person will be better equipped as an adult to favorably transform some, if not all, the undesirable traits.

Parents, please do not despair! As mere imperfect humans, you cannot be entirely infallible in the parenting role. However, if you realize the importance of the role and put forth unselfish efforts toward being the best parent possible, you are on the right road. You must give your children great dosages of love together with an awareness of those limitations that cannot be trespassed. You must insist on the respect required as a deterrent for improper conduct. If you can keep this balance of love, respect and discipline, you will have contributed immensely toward creating a happy and stable adult even if some minor mistakes were made along the way.

This chapter is dedicated to the importance of being good parents, but in the big scheme of attaining your individual happiness, if you were not fortunate to have had good parents, it is now your responsibility as adults to put the blame game away and correct the damage. You must attempt to master the outlined principles in each chapter to the degree that you can which, with God's help, will gradually allow you to repair whatever problems you may have originating from your childhood.

Although I was not as aware as I am today of the far reaching and lasting effects we could cause on our children, we raised two fine girls through instinctive motherly and fatherly love and dedication probably instilled in us by our own parents. Based on my own experience here are some simple pointers to parents that can help in your parenting efforts.

- Give your children all the love you can in every way possible. Discipline is important, but when in doubt in a particular situation, I believe it is better to give an overdose of love than of discipline. An overdose of love perhaps may produce some spoiling for a while, depending on the child's natural traits. However, when that child begins to mature into an adult, its chances of becoming a well-adjusted person are greater, with a large reservoir of love, than a child who has been over disciplined with insufficient love to balance the equation. The ideal situation, naturally, is a balance of much love with appropriate discipline and firmness, when necessary. This balance is what all parents should strive to achieve because a child who knows, without a doubt, that it is loved unconditionally, accepts discipline when it knows way deep it was deserved. In contrast, a child wanting in love sees discipline as one more sign of lack of love and resents it bitterly even when the child may apparently accept it.

- Talk to your children, praise them, play with them, touch them, cuddle them comfort them when they are anxious, afraid or hurt.
- Never treat your children with loud and vile language and lack of respect. Treat them with the same respect you wish to instill in them. They are great imitators and learn more by example than words.
- Since we have established that all children are not the same, and some have better or worse personality traits, realistically evaluate your child in this respect, and focus your parenting to help improve the undesirable traits.
- Do not allow lack of respect under any circumstance.
- Be consistent to ignore their attempts to manipulate by sticking firmly to your resolve of having them do what they must do.
- Boost your children's self-esteem by praising all of their achievements, big or small, and by encouraging them when

they are lacking in some ability. Do not demand of them more than they can give, but stimulate them to give their best, whatever that may be.

- Accept your children as they are—with some virtues and some faults, with some abilities and some lack of abilities. Do not criticize them, but guide and encourage them to improve.
- Do not embarrass your children in front of others. If they must be reprimanded, do so quietly, alone, with firmness, but also with respect.
- Trust them and show them you believe them worthy of being trusted. This applies to those children who have not displayed a natural trait to lie. For those who tend to lie, trust has to be won by their actions.
- Always be there when they need you. Parents are the only persons in the world on which a child can rely in any condition— a great and reassuring feeling to have when no one else seems to care or understand.
- Establish free communication with your children so you can always know what is going on in their young minds. You should always be understanding parents, capable of listening, and showing genuine interest in what they have to tell you so they will keep you tuned in.
- Keep young at heart and grow with your children. Times change and parents must not remain static and inflexible, following a fixed pattern which was perhaps adequate when you were growing up, but is not necessarily so today.
- Make your home the center of love and fun. You should welcome their friends, and let them have pets and freedom to play even if it means a not so impeccably clean house. It is

much better to have a messy house full of children and toys than a play-deprived child who will always resent that part of its childhood. Let your children get dirty at play. Clothes can be washed, and a good bath will put them in top shape again, but you will not get another chance to let them have a happy and fun-filled childhood.

- Do not be overprotective. Allow your children to develop and to experiment as they grow. Usually when parents protect their children excessively, they do so only to avoid worrying about their children if they are involved in whatever the parents themselves fear. It is easier to not allow your child to do something you fear than to allow the child to develop even though it causes you much worry. My advice is to let your children do everything they should do, step by step along the way as they grow, and just do a lot of praying over your fears.

- Through a good husband/wife relationship that reflects love, physical attraction, and respect, allow your children to learn about such a meaningful relationship as marriage giving them a true and vivid example which they will later imitate in their own adult relationship as husbands or wives.

- Do not hit your children. Physical punishment is used only because it is easier and requires no intellectual involvement while at the same time affording the parents the chance to release their anger. Parents who resort to physical punishment when they are angry or embarrassed over a child's behavior, generally do so because they know their children have no alternative but to take it. We can get just as angry or upset with husbands, wives, friends, or bosses, but we contain ourselves and refrain from hitting them, primarily because we know we cannot get away with it. Besides, there is the probability that we could get hit back. This probability does not exist with our youngsters. With them we can feel superior and unchallenged, and in the name of discipline, we justify and unleash our violence and hostility on our children who can do nothing but cry and accept. Perhaps, the parent is simply duplicating the kind of treatment the parent received as a child. Physical punishment is unfair because nothing our children may do warrants it when there are so many other options. We should not take the easy way out, but use intelligence, patience and firmness in correcting the wrongdoing.

I believe there can be an exception to the above. A parent may need to spank a child without being violent as an immediate warning in the event of an urgent dangerous situation such as crossing a street without supervision, jumping from a tall tree or balcony and the like. The purpose of this action is to detain but not to inflict true physical hurt. I do not consider as physical punishment a quick light spank aimed to deter an unacceptable action.

In summation, if as an individual you may have been affected by poor parenting or parenting errors, please continue forward with the ultimate mission of achieving happiness for yourself and for your children because a happy person will inevitably be a better parent. Please endeavor to be the very best you can be in this important role of people molding realizing the tremendous far-reaching power you possess.

CHAPTER 17

Words To Future Parents

Reality is that most of us have been negatively affected by our parents in one way or another, to a greater or lesser degree. We have no alternative now but to help ourselves by recognizing and understanding our negative feelings and behavior and correcting these without further self-pity. It is too late to blame our parents for mistakes they might have made. Now, the job is yours. You must do it yourselves.

Many of us have already parented our own children, and perhaps made some mistakes that are also beyond repair. We can only wish that these were minimal and that our children will also help themselves rather than sit back and blame us. But, there is still time for future parents to become better prepared for this gigantic role. It is to them that I dedicate these words with the hope that I might strike a note of awareness and urgency in their minds and hearts.

It is absolutely essential that all women and men contemplating to become parents realize exactly the potential power they possess when they decide to assume this responsibility. There is much fun in preparing to become a parent. There is the layette, buying all those pretty baby things, selecting the baby furniture and planning the nursery, the baby showers, and choosing the baby's name as well as all the extra attention the expecting mother gets from her husband and others. All of these things should be enjoyed and should put you, the future parents, in the right frame of mind. They should create in you the appropriate attitude of enthusiasm that should prevail in assuming such a beautiful role as parenthood. But, there is much more to be done.

You must also prepare in a more serious and deeper way by understanding exactly and truly what parenthood means when it is stripped of all the superficial and glamorous elements. What is left is the bare reality that you will have in your hands a small baby whose future two to four years of life will be almost totally in your hands and influenced by you. You need to be cognizant that this influence will be carried through the person's later life and in effect will determine, to a great degree, whether this baby will be a happy or an unhappy person. Now, this is a tremendous responsibility, and future parents should prepare for it. You need to be ready to meet this challenge so that when that adorable baby arrives, you will not only enjoy all the fun that undoubtedly you will have with your baby, but you will also be fully aware of your important part in shaping its life. Knowing exactly what is expected of you is totally necessary as you begin to mold this new life in a positive way through love and dedication.

I am not a psychologist and am not qualified to go into the subject professionally. Therefore, my recommendation to future parents is to read good books written by experts in the field that can guide you on how to face the parenting problems you may encounter. I would also encourage you to enroll in special courses designed to help you achieve a good parent/child relationship.

In addition to seeking as much knowledge as possible from professionals, I would like to point out some proven guidelines offered in the previous chapter which were inspired by our own experience as parents. These simple, non professional, common sense rules are born from normal intuitive child raising and could help you.

As I close this chapter I wish to leave this thought for those of you who are not yet parents but who will soon be or may be in the future:

You will become the most powerful person on earth in that baby's life for quite some time. As such, you will be able to create or destroy a child's emotional makeup. Please, do not let your child, yourself, and the world down as you assume this role of roles.

CHAPTER 18

The Quest For Happiness Of The Working Woman And Mate

Because I have worked outside the home practically all of my life, I have a special spot in my heart for the woman with a husband or mate and family who face the outside world each working day. Despite the tension and demands to which she is exposed, she still manages to meet her many responsibilities to her partner, her children and herself. In the larger scheme of finding happiness, individually or in marriage, I believe it is important to understand the various choices related to work that will affect not only the working woman's happiness but also that of her husband or mate and her children. For this reason, this chapter is of interest not only to all working women but also to their husbands or mates.

To explore the challenges of the woman who works outside the home, we must distinguish the various kinds of working women because although most have much in common, each has different demands and objectives. Primarily, they can be divided as:

- the single woman
- the single mother
- the woman with a husband or mate (which I shall call wife heretofore) with or without children

Analyzing each, we know that:
- Both the single woman as well as the single mother generally do not have a choice whether to work or not. In most cases they both must work for their livelihood unless they happen to be of a wealthy family or have financial support from another source. They may work at a job or be a business or career woman. The single mother, a true heroin, must work in her dual role as mother and father with zero help from a husband or mate.
- The wife with or without children may choose not to work, depending on what she and her husband or mate decide. This choice should be reached together because it plays a very important part in the happiness of both partners and that of the children. Therefore, the choice to work or not should be weighed very carefully.

The working wife with or without children can be further divided into those who choose to work in a regular job or who are business or career women primarily for the following reasons:
- They prefer working at a job or to be engaged in business or in their career because the activity fulfills them more than their domestic duties;
- They work primarily to contribute to the family economy. However, they would prefer staying at home as a housewife.

My heart goes out more to this kind who, while putting forth efforts to help and boost the family finances, leaves an important part of her soul at home, where she would prefer to be;
- They work to help the family financially but at the same time find fulfillment in their work or business or career. This is a more fortunate variation.

It is important to note that in all cases, most working wives try to perform well their various roles, while keeping up with the exigencies of their jobs, business, and careers.

In this chapter I have concentrated to a greater extent on the working wife with or without children and the single mother because their work activity has a greater impact on others in their lives. Both the working wife with children and the single mother face similar difficult demands except that the single mother must face these demands without help from a husband or mate. However, although handicapped by having to handle her responsibilities alone, she does not have to contend with the demands of a husband or mate.

The working wife with children and the single mother are a brand of women that deserves special recognition. Their very difficult role is not quite understood by housewives and mothers who have never worked outside the home. While physically away from home a great part of the day, they can quickly change from the outside world, that same world that men face, and transform themselves into efficient homemakers, homework helpers, and loving mothers. The working wife with children must also be an understanding and caring wife. These women are capable of putting aside their own tense feelings from a day of outside activities and discard the problems they may have encountered during their day to become good wives and mothers.

Having been one of these versatile females myself, I know well how difficult this role can be. I commend the ability of the working wife with children and the single mother to accomplish so much using resources that many stay-at-home wives and mothers have never had to tap.

Regardless of what propels wives to engage in working activities outside the home, and regardless of how satisfied or unsatisfied they may be with their outside activities, the fact remains that they have multiple special duties facing them. They are confronted with many demands unknown to the married woman who remains at home. Ironically, many housewives consider the working wife as a more self-sufficient liberated woman who is privileged to break with the drudgery of their seemingly uninteresting life of domesticity. They admire the working wife who has her own money without having to ask her husband or mate. They envision the working wife with a more glamorous life, wearing nicer clothes every day instead of their usual everyday attire of faded shorts, jeans or housecoat. The housewife sees her working counterpart as having lunch out with the girls and being totally free from the uneventful routine of housework. This aura of glamour surrounding the working wife, as seen by the housewife, would immediately dissipate if they were to see their supposedly more privileged companions in real action when they get home.

There are marked differences between the working wife, the single mother and the housewife. The housewife has more flexibility to adjust her work schedule and requirements to jive with her capabilities on a given day, and can linger five or ten minutes longer over coffee. The working wife with or without children and the single mother have to get up each work morning, rain or shine, with menstrual pains or piercing headache, and get ready, watching the clock closely for every minute is precious. There is a schedule to be met, and just a few minutes can make her late. Once at work, these women have to contemporize and get along with multiple personalities while the housewife is the Queen Bee of her hive. The working wife and the single mother who work at a job have to deal not only with the big boss but usually with other smaller supervisors and coworkers as well. Unfortunately, many times some of these people have difficult personalities, but she must learn to cope and to solve the problems that might arise so she can survive and keep her job.

Something as simple and basic as desperately wanting to go to the bathroom sometimes just has to wait. Maybe, she would like to just stretch out for a few minutes or take a short nap, but that is totally out of the question. Some days the working wife and the single mother have personal problems weighing over them, but the show must go on. They have other personal problems to solve like doctor, dental and other appointments not only for themselves but also for the children which they must try to work in at lunch or on Saturdays or day off—-those precious weekends or days off that mean so much to these women. They practically plan and live from days off to days off, cramming everything into them from hairdresser, shopping, to housecleaning, washing, and even fun.

The working wife with children and the single mother cannot indulge in partying during a work day. They are aware they have to be up early the next day alert and ready to meet the requirements of their jobs and family. Out there in that work and business jungle, the working wife and the single mother find it difficult sometimes to even make a short personal call. Their entire personal life has to wait, to be put on hold and lived in the five to six hours they will have during the evening.

Some working wives with children and single mothers have to wake up at dawn to get everything ready so they can drive their small children to the nursery in time to make it punctually to work. In the afternoon they must go through the same running around in reverse. Later, when they get home, totally exhausted, they usually must assume most of the same domestic duties of the all-day housewife. They just have to do them in less time and under more pressure. Their children still look upon them as the mother who has to listen to their problems and help them and guide them with their schoolwork. At times they may even attend PTA meetings rushing through the front door with just enough time to maybe freshen up or grab a bite to get to school in time.

The working wife has additional requirements. She is still regarded by her soul-mate as his woman who should be relaxed, should prepare him a decent meal, should provide him with clean clothes and a presentable home, and perhaps give him a bit of romantic action later in the evening. The working wife does not have time for bubble baths before her husband or mate gets home, and it is much more difficult for her to be the sweet understanding wife her partner may expect.

Since I was a working wife, I feel qualified to analyze the complex life of the working wife with or without children and to denounce the myth that exists in the minds of wives and mothers who have not worked outside the home. There is much to be said for the working wife with or without children because there are times when she must intelligently mask and restrain her acquired initiative and aggressiveness and pretend she is the helpless woman her husband/mate would prefer at that moment. It takes a great deal more doing for a working wife who contributes financially to the household to forget about her own bad day at work and convert into the docile wife her husband or mate would like to find when he gets home tired and upset with his own bag of problems.

Despite all that is expected of her, we know that most working women are great wives and mothers, and in some cases, do a better job in these roles than women who have much more time and less pressure. I know this is possible because we are all capable of much more than we think. If a sincere and earnest desire exists, women can do just about anything they set their minds and hearts to do. I have found that working wives and single mothers value their scarce time so much that they have learned to use their time much more efficiently than many of the stay-at-home counterparts.

Working wives and single mothers are more practical and take shortcuts, eliminate many unnecessary chores, and under pressure accomplish more. The housewife who regards each day as hers to plan, control, and do, knowing that what she cannot accomplish today, she can tackle tomorrow, or the next day, or the next, tends sometimes to work at a slower pace. Hence she often does less than the working wife or the single mother who is forced to organize herself so that every free minute will count. The working wife and the single mother cook ahead for the week, they freeze meals, they clean at night, and use their lunch hour to write checks or shop quickly. They do not wash every day or fuss too much over trivial chores, but plan, plan, plan. They have to, or they will just not make it, and being everything they want to be means too much for them to relent. The working wife and single mother have the drive to achieve, developed by their desire to be successful in their various roles, which is one of the greatest assets they acquire from their rigorous schedule.

Like in every situation there are always pros and cons. So far, I have elaborated only on the demands and problems of the working wife with or without children and those of the single mother. However, the working wife with or without a family undoubtedly has also many benefits that can accrue to her if she is wise and learns to take advantage of them. A working wife can be a better wife because of it. Because she associates and mingles with other men, she should better understand her husband. She is in a better position to become informed in a diversity of subjects and therefore be a more interesting companion for her husband as opposed to stay-home wives who sometimes do not keep up with current happenings outside their domestic kingdom. The working wife usually keeps up more with fashions and fads, watches her weight more, and generally looks younger. There are exceptions, but generally speaking, many women that stay home are not as careful of their appearance as those that go outside the home to engage in outside activities.

The working wife is usually a more useful mate for today's man who is more capable of viewing competence in his woman as an asset instead of a challenge. She can handle many more things for her husband or mate who learns to rely on her much more in areas where many times the housewife does not become involved. In this world with a super abundance of women, the working wife who is sharp and makes herself as attractive, appealing, and intelligent as the women with whom her husband is exposed is in a better position to be viewed by her husband at par with them.

In the area of motherhood, the working mother, single or married, who cares and tries a little harder also has advantages. Because most working mothers tend to have guilty feelings about not devoting as much time to the children as they feel they should or would like, they will go to all ends to make up for the deficiency by dedicating much more of themselves in the shorter time they spend with their children. Whereas, the mother who is home all day with her children may exhaust her patience more quickly or even rejoice when she can get them off to grandma's or in bed early. Many times, she does not truly value the wonderful opportunity she has of being with them all day. In contrast, the working mother, in an effort to compensate for the time she does not spend with the children, becomes a super-mother when she is with them, planning outings and activities with them. It is not uncommon for the children of working mothers to consider their working Moms as special. In contrast, children and mothers who spend all day together often can get on each other's nerves.

Of course, this is a subject on which we cannot generalize because not all women are the same nor need the same stimulants. There are some very patient non-working mothers who have a natural ability and gift to care for children, do a beautiful job and never seem to tire or wish to be relieved. However, non working mothers who do not have that special gift could possibly benefit from becoming working mothers. They might just be excellent mothers when the time spent with the children is shorter and much more precious for both.

Fortunately for today's working wives with children, men are now much more aware and conscious of the heavy schedule their wives carry, and they are more considerate of their working mates, lending a hand so that the wives' burden becomes less excessive. Most working wives are successful in communicating their problems to their husbands and enlisting their help without hostility or resentment. The husband/mate support is a must for this arrangement to work properly in a marriage, and the partners must be in total agreement before it is entered. The pros and cons must be realistically discussed. The wife and husband or mate must have a frank discussion on this important decision to better evaluate whether working outside the home, for whatever reason, will be detrimental to the marriage and the family. This is an important decision to be made jointly because it would be far better to do without some material things if in return the family relationship is happier. Each case is different and unique, depending on the husband's aspirations and personality, the children's age, the quality and availability of a mother substitute and the wife's capacity to meet the versatile and heavy demands that she will have to face if she wishes to play all her roles well.

Words of admonition for the woman who works or is engaged in business or career activities only for self fulfillment.

When a woman works only for self-fulfillment, the situation is somewhat different because along with all of the other factors to be considered, she must also think of herself as an individual and on how much this fulfillment means to her. Personally, I believe that under no circumstance should she perform poorly as mother or wife just for the sake of self fulfillment. Ultimately she will find that the satisfaction and realization she will derive will not provide sufficient happiness to compensate for her failure in these two ultra-important roles which she voluntarily assumed. Therefore, in thinking of her needs as she should, she must also realize that in addition to achieving self-fulfillment, she needs to find fulfillment as wife and mother and be the best she can be in all her womanly facets. This is probably not easy for the woman who values self fulfillment to an extreme.

I believe that the woman seeking primarily her own fulfillment in whatever outside activity she engages must also develop a desire for fulfillment in her other important roles, if she is to attain happiness. As a wife and mother, she needs to create a happy and lasting marriage or relationship for herself, husband or mate as well as for the children. She also needs to perform well in her role of shaping and molding into a happy life those children she willingly brought into this world and who are now one of her greatest responsibilities. If she is unable to obtain fulfillment from being a good wife and mother and can only find fulfillment in her outside activities, her probabilities of finding true happiness are much more difficult. She risks feeling incomplete and empty only with personal fulfillment.

The demands on the woman who must have self-fulfillment, completely independent of being a wife and mother, are much heavier. She will have to pay a premium for her personal fulfillment in her work, business or career by having to excel as a wife and mother also. If she is able to achieve this excellence, she will also receive in return much more satisfaction from having performed all her roles well. This follows the reasoning: if you want more, you must pay more.

The woman who needs self-fulfillment must keep in mind that she assumed multiple responsibilities when she decided to become a wife, a mother, as well as a working woman or a career or business woman. There is no question but that it is a tremendous feat for her to excel in her diverse responsibilities. **But,**

it can be done. If she is not willing to put forth the extra efforts required of her in meeting her combined goals and is convinced that her personal fulfillment is more important, she should probably not marry or assume the responsibility of motherhood. She would be cheating her husband and children unfairly. For her unwillingness to give more, she should accept life with her personal fulfillment alone and not create other responsibilities and commitments that deserve more from her than she is willing to give.

I started working when I was 17, while attending the University of Tampa for a two-year Secretarial Sciences Certificate, and from that day forward, I have always been a working woman. At 18, when we married, I continued working because we needed the financial help and because we did not plan children right away. Later, with each promotion and raise, I became hooked on the extra income that allowed us many pleasures and extras without undue sacrifice on my part because I had outside help that made the domestic demand on me quite doable. When the children came, we always had a positive factor in our favor with the availability of a built-in baby sitter in my mother-in-law first and in my mother later. Therefore, my decision to continue taking advantage of the salary I could command was much easier to make because I knew that my girls were in very good hands during week days, with much love and care from their grandmothers. When I came home, I became that extra special, extra loving mother. The girls saw me more as a fun Mommy who would always do things with them, did not lose her temper and had patience in dealing with them. I don't think either of my girls was unfavorably affected by my working activities because of the combination of grandmother love during the day and the super mother love and care I showered upon them when I was with them.

As a working wife, I think I managed quite well also. From the very beginning, Jay and I discussed the working decision, and we agreed there would never be "my money" and "your money" but "our money." For all of our 66 years of marriage we have deposited jointly, figured our budget jointly, and spent our money on what we jointly decided. Never once did I ever make my husband feel that I considered myself economically independent or justified in buying something because it was my money. I have always believed that when couples handle their monies independently, there is a financial separation that can lead to friction and problems in the marriage or relationship if the wife also works. We both agreed that I would work, and we analyzed and understood that the motivation behind the decision was never based on my achieving economic independence. Therefore, it was only equitable to pool our incomes, and to jointly decide on how we wanted to use the money, without distinction of whose money would be used for what purpose. It has worked very well for us, and I recommend this arrangement to avoid conflicts when the woman contributes equally to the household economy.

Jay has always been good at pitching in and helping around the house when I have needed him. From the very first days of our marriage, we always talked about sharing, and Jay very early in the marriage learned to live with a working wife without demanding unduly of her. In turn, because of his unselfishness and consideration through the years, I also learned to be as much like a non-working wife as I humanly could so that he would not miss being catered to or feel I was so busy or tense that there was little or no time for conversation and love. We both took extra care to make the arrangement work and perhaps paid the price with a certain amount of extra sacrifice, but the reward we received of a happy marriage was well worth the price. As with all things, you must work at happiness. Nothing ever comes easy or by your lucky stars.

I believe that the man who has agreed to have his wife work should exercise understanding and show extra special consideration to the woman who, with his approval, faces the outside world just as he, and still attempts to be a loving and good wife and mother. He must realize the magnitude of the challenge she is confronting.

I always had the awareness that many men, consciously or subconsciously, harbor secret resentment and mixed feelings about having their wives work. I also realized that although Jay was in agreement that our arrangement was quite workable, and he was perfectly willing to cooperate in every way, it was important for him to command a larger income that would give me the option to stay at home, if I preferred. My working purely for financial reasons and not out of choice clearly meant to him that I worked because he was not capable of making it alone. This bothered him much more than adapting to the arrangement in any other way. I could sense these feelings in him whenever the subject came up, especially when at times I expressed a desire to stay home. I realized it was important for me to change the negative feeling in him, and we had a good talk. I assured him sincerely that I was happy at my job because it was interesting, fulfilling and well paid.

In later years when we reached a stage in our finances in which my income was not necessary to meet our basic budget, I accepted the responsibility for continuing on the job because I was a big spender with a perennial project in mind. I made it totally clear that working was the penalty I was willing to pay for my enthusiastic life style of living here and now. Using my feminine intuition, we worked it out quite well.

Again, as I have pointed out before, the working wife has the ability to do so much to minimize most problems by using tact and intelligence. In each particular case, the working wife can handle wisely the special problems that might arise in their arrangement so that the husband will not have feelings of inadequacy as a provider nor feel he has been cheated of attention and love because of his wife's busy schedule. It is to the working wife's benefit to apply altruistic egotism and to enlist the Lord's guidance in making her role as a working wife as appealing as possible to her husband. Doing so will pay off in a happier relationship whether the wife is working out of choice or financial need.

As I end this chapter, I wish to make clear that in praising the working wife, I am not undermining the housewife in any way. She has a tremendous job to accomplish and should be proud of her important and natural role. The housewife should experience much fulfillment in doing her job well because she truly is in a perfect position to make her home everything it should be for her husband, children, and herself.

Without taking away from the merits of the housewife, I toast with admiration and respect the tough breed of women who are champions in giving their all to their partners and children in an amazing balancing act as wives and mothers while still retaining their individuality as women.

CHAPTER 19

As You Up In Years, Stay Young At Heart

The older years bring changes coupled with blessings. It is a time to re-evaluate your new life, your new goals, your new priorities, your new interests and your new challenges. This new stage of life offers more leisure and fewer responsibilities. You need to learn how to enjoy these new privileges that you have earned. You must also resolve to continue being active physically and mentally, so that these special years bring you the blessing of good health and well being.

In this chapter, I am also focusing on an important challenge that you will probably need to address because it will affect your happiness and that of your adult children: your position as the mature parents of adult children.

As you become mature parents of adult children, you need much wisdom and a selfless analysis of who you are at this given point and time. If you have lived life to the fullest, as you should have, and did those things that you should have done when you were young, and if you were the key figure of your home during the years your children were growing, then you should be ready to relinquish this Numero

Uno position to your adult children and pass on the baton. They are now at the prime of their lives and have the right to enjoy the privilege of living their own lives, just as you did.

Nothing can make mature parents more unpopular with their adult children than trying to have them live by your standards and not allowing them to learn by their own experiences and mistakes. Experience is great. Nothing can quite substitute it, but it belongs only to those who have acquired it by living and experimenting with life. Unfortunately, experience cannot be passed on to the young because it can only come from living. Your adult children have the right to gain experience for themselves. True, they will probably make mistakes you wish you could have them avoid, but you cannot hamper their natural desire to try and discover life for themselves. They would always resent this well-intended protectiveness on your part. As parents of adult children you must simply stand by, hoping you have done the job well of creating happy stable adults and watch them experience the same things you did, praying that God will guide them in the right direction. Only then will you find a place in your adult children's lives.

They will want to invite you to share with them because Mom and Dad are not interfering, critical nagging older persons who attempt to live their lives for them. Mom and Dad are cool! As much as our children may love you, they will only politely ask you on occasions, and you will feel excluded from their lives, if you choose to continue playing the same predominant part in their lives that you did when they were children. But, if you are intelligent and cognizant that it is their turn to live and can gracefully step down to a secondary position in their lives, you will always remain close to them and will be welcome company in their homes. That should be your goal as mature parents!

As you up in years, you must remain young at heart and change with the times. You cannot become stagnant and incapable of assimilating or understanding new ideas and concepts. This does not mean you have to practice them yourself if they are not natural to you. Many times, you can never quite approve them, but you must condone them in the young, just as years ago our ideas and concepts were quite different from those of our parents and grandparents. Life goes on perpetually evolving, and you must evolve with it.

Remember when you were at your prime how you decided what time dinner would be served, what would be cooked, and whether to invite friends over. Every decision of how you chose to live and rule in your homes was yours to make, but now you can continue to exercise this power only in your own homes— —not in your children's. Your adult children's home is their domain, and if they choose not to make beds or do the dishes or eat dinner at midnight, much as you may be shocked, you have no jurisdiction over the way they wish to live. The sooner you realize and accept this fact, the sooner you will be happy mature parents, contributing toward your adult children's happiness as well.

Often, widowed mothers are brought to live with their adult children because their children worry about their loneliness or financial situation. In Hispanic families, such as mine, it is customary for the older folks to live with their children, and when the grandchildren arrive, there is a merge of three generations in one household. This could be beautiful and beneficial to all, if the older generation is willing to relinquish and step aside. However, if your maturity has not reached the level needed to understand that you are living in your children's home, not yours, it would be much better not to attempt this togetherness. When older parents can assume their less dominant place in the household, the result can be productive and helpful to everyone. The mature parents will feel needed, and they will be able to enjoy the fun and love that inevitably exists around the younger set instead of aging alone and oftentimes dying of loneliness rather than of any physical ailment. The adult children can enjoy having built-in baby sitters, and a sense of happiness derived from knowing they are taking care of their older parents just as they took care of them when they were frail and helpless babies. The grandchildren can grow up in an atmosphere of extra love that only grandparents can offer because they are no longer responsible for their discipline and can just enjoy them.

This is one beautiful package, as it should and could be, but unfortunately, sometimes, this generational mix does not work mainly because older parents are not intelligent and refuse to accept their secondary place in the household. They are offered love and companionship but not the right to make decisions or intervene in any way with how the adult children manage their lives and homes. They can only be passive bystanders and should not deviate from this role if they wish to live with their adult children.

This brings us to an all important decision this stage of life demands. You need to ask yourselves what do you really want in your later years. Do you want companionship and togetherness because you fear loneliness even at the expense of giving up your independence? Do you wish to continue being vital and independent in your own home, foregoing loneliness and companionship? You must truly know yourself, and honestly answer these questions. If you know you are independent or domineering, you should never attempt to live with your adult children regardless of how lonely you may feel at times. It is much better to be welcomed at your children's homes as a passing visitor, and to call on them when you need them, and vice versa, then to live together unhappily if taking a secondary passive role is truly a sacrifice for you. If you are determined to continue being in charge of your life, you should not choose to live with your adult children.

We have been independent mature parents for many years. God has blessed us so that in our 80s we still have each other, and our health has held up so that we function well on our own, and have a happy independent life. Although we are independent, we can always count on our family, if needed, and we have also been able to help our family in many ways. Our home has been a haven for our family, and our doors are always open to them.

We have picked up grandchildren from school and taken in adult grandchildren when they have needed temporary help just out of college and before marrying. We have even been able to help take care of the great grandchildren at times and have built a close bond with them which is priceless. Our spacious van has always been at the disposal of the family when needed to haul large objects. We were able to provide storage space in our extra guest room for our son Oscar's antique record players as he built up this side business. I assist our adult children and grandchildren in solving problems that require online help and phone calling that they pass on to me because of their busy schedules. I pride myself to still be able to help in things of this nature which is not very typical for 80+ mothers and grandmothers.

Just recently we opened our home to our daughter and son, Adele and Stan, so they could make the transition from Chicago to Miami and be closer to their grandchildren. God has blessed us by allowing us to still be helpful to our family while maintaining our independence.

Both our daughters have been married for many years, and although they live their own lives with their husbands and family, we have always been close and have been included in many of their travel and activities. We have spent long vacations with Adele and Stan when they lived in Mexico and in various other places. We have enjoyed our time with them, always assuming a secondary role while in their homes. I would say that the best proof we have had that we have done well as mature parents has been Stan's affectionate invitations to visit and to stay longer. They have truly made us feel welcome, and we are quite proud of this. We have also enjoyed many jointly planned trips with Annette and Oscar including many beach vacations. In all our times at their homes or on trips, we have exercised wisdom and tact to make ourselves good company and to never assume an assertive role as mature parents.

Our family tells us we are fun because we have kept young at heart. We never dampen their enthusiasm with criticism or censor any of their actions. As a result, they always tell us about their projects and plans. We remember our own many years before and can relate to their enthusiasm. As older parents, we savor their excitement with happiness. It has taken years of living to bring us to our maturity, and it is unfair to expect them to reach the same maturity without having had the chance of living those years themselves. In total, if you are mature parents of adult children and wish to be popular with them and to have them want you as part of their lives, let them live their own lives, let them learn by their own mistakes, encourage them, love them, and just be good company. Keep all criticism to yourself, and be able to relinquish the No. 1 position that was yours when they were youngsters. It is their time now.

At this new stage of life, you have new advantages that you need to discover and enjoy. You have acquired much experience that helps you in many ways to live more peacefully and happily. You can handle your problems much more effectively because you have more time and less pressure. You are not bombarded with the tension that comes with meeting deadlines and responsibilities. With maturity come knowledge, contentment, understanding, and the ability to truly love without possessiveness. With these acquired gifts, your life as you up in years will be beautiful, interesting and enjoyable if you continue to grow and remain spiritually young.

Above all, my message is to stay young at heart. Ever really listened to the lyrics of that song? If you have not, I recommend it. It delivers the message so eloquently.

CHAPTER 20

Don't Tell Me You Can't Change

Throughout I have pointed out numerous attitudes and principles that can bring happiness to our lives. In most cases, I have illustrated with actual experiences how these attitudes and principles can work to our benefit and demonstrated they are achievable and far from impossible to develop. I have emphasized the importance of connecting with God as your friend, counselor, teacher, with total faith. Now, there is nothing more to be said; now is the hour of truth. It is your choice to be happy or unhappy. It is entirely up to you to follow my way to happiness .

If you wish to sit back, feel miserable with yourself, talk about your problems over and over again, but do nothing more, you will probably always be unhappy. If after recognizing and understanding the available solutions, you still decide to accept your unhappiness, instead of taking conscious action to change wherever change is needed, then perhaps you do not deserve to be happy. How sad!

You will be tossing away a fantastic opportunity to discover joy, contentment and peace of mind in a lasting way if you convince yourself that you cannot change, This would be tragic because there is so much at stake for you. Reading all the books in the world on happiness cannot make you happy. It takes positive action on your part, and no one can change you but you yourself.

Some persons have told me how aware they are of their personality faults such as a fiery temper, lack of persistency, pessimism, inability to be content with the small joys of life and so on. They just cannot change, they tell me. They argue and try to convince themselves that this is the way they are, that life has dealt them a tough hand, and there is nothing they can do about it. I cannot help but feel upset when I hear unhappy people reason this way. Yes, it is tough, but mostly for them who will continue being miserable because of their lack of guts to change whatever is causing their unhappiness.

Often, I have sensed a touch of pride in some of these people when they say that they cannot help themselves because they are who they are as if they consider themselves in a class of their own that should be accepted "as is". They seem to be implying: "I've got to be me, regardless, and you must accept me as I am". They fail to realize that no one has to accept a person with undesirable traits. If they are unhappy by being "me," even if others were willing to put up with them and their unfavorable and negative attitudes, they still have to live with themselves. The primary reason why they should change is not to make others accept them, but to make themselves happy as they overcome their undesirable attitudes and traits. The goal is personal although others will benefit from the changed attitude.

If you are truly happy with yourself, you should not change just to conform to someone else's demands and expectations. There is a distinction to be made in these cases. If the change in you that is needed is attainable without creating unhappiness for you and can add to your happiness by making life easier for you in your relationship with others, then you should try to change so that you can be even happier. However, if having a better relationship with others is not important to you, and you genuinely feel happy with yourself "as is," by all means, do not change what works for you.

You must weigh if the beauty of being you, the individual, interferes with something far superior, the beauty of being happy, profoundly, serenely and permanently, then you should view this as your primary goal. This is the kind of happiness that everyone appears to be seeking. The problem lies in that many feel it can be achieved effortlessly. Never once have I said or implied that changing long-time ingrained traits and attitudes is easy, but yes possible, if you persist and persist. Regardless of how you spin it, all philosophy involving happiness entails some change in our attitudes because happiness in itself is one huge attitude that encompasses many smaller ones.

For some persons, less effort is required because of their natural traits and/or a more desirable childhood, but we all have some area in which we can improve or change. No one is born perfect or had an absolutely perfect childhood, nor will anyone achieve perfection either. But, all of us can help ourselves to some degree. Perhaps, a terribly fiery temper can be controlled only to some degree, but whatever you achieve will make you that much happier. Maybe at first, you are able to make only a mere small improvement, but by not giving up, and by seeing the benefits even this small improvement brings you, you will probably be encouraged to try harder for more change. After some time, you will see that you are no longer the hot irate person that you were, and even though, you will probably always have a lower boiling point than a naturally easy-going person, you are now able to control your anger and live more pleasantly with yourself and others.

One thing I know is that happiness does exist, that it is attainable, and that it can be yours. You must remember that happiness brings with it many beautiful feelings. It brings a feeling of satisfaction with yourself and life, it gives you a sense of contentment with many things, it lets you truly love and be capable of giving happiness to others, it allows you to feel joy with the many small things around you, it lets you recognize your many blessings, and it helps you learn to put your problems in perspective. You need to work at changing the negative attitudes in you that prevent you from these wonderful feelings. I am not alone in this belief. I am a happy person, and I know others like me. Maybe you will have to try a little more, maybe not, but I know that changing undesirable attitudes is worth the sacrifice, difficult as it may be.

You should be satisfied with whatever achievement you make, and be patient with yourself when you think you have not made progress. Hang in and never, never give up. You must keep trying because with each small victory, your outlook will change and improve, and you will see happiness seeping through as you create it with your changed attitudes. You will gain confidence in your ability to be happier and will make further changes, gradually becoming the happy person you want to be.

To recap, you should put forth efforts to improve on these principles:

- Love yourself and others.
- Show your love and admiration to others. Loving is not enough.
- Be tolerant and kind to others. Do not discriminate.
- Count your blessings and enjoy all the wonderful small things around you.

- With optimism and enthusiasm work to make your dreams come true.
- Avoid boredom by keeping busy and productive.
- Be quick to apologize for your errors.
- Don't be supersensitive.
- Control that temper.
- Live today to the fullest, forget yesterday, and don't worry too much about tomorrow.
- Keep God in your life, pray always, ask, seek, and knock at His door when you have problems believing He is listening.
- If you are married or in a significant relationship, work at achieving a happy marriage and union with mutual love, respect, compromise, and admiration.
- If you are a parent, assume the important task of people molding with love, awareness and dedication.
- If you are a working woman, wife and mother, do the utmost to perform with excellence each role.
- Stay young at heart as you up in years and learn to be the mature parent of adult children.

And finally, enlisting God's help through prayer, work relentlessly at removing obstacles from your life and changing whatever attitude is preventing you from being happy which is the goal we all are seeking.

These are big goals that will contribute to your happiness which is one immense goal. As you become a happy person, you will add much happiness to the world by adding happiness to everyone you touch, by making your marriage and relationship happy and lasting, by striving to shape your children into happy persons, and by giving them the foundation they will need to continue working at this goal of goals, All of the beautiful principles outlined in this book can be achieved, to a greater or lesser degree, if you are willing to change. It is your choice from here on, and the only thing left to say is:

DON'T TELL ME YOU CAN'T CHANGE!
If others can do it, you can too, so with God as your partner, let's get started on the way to happiness. Your journey will be as beautiful as mine has been!

CPSIA information can be obtained at www.ICGtesting.com
Printed in the USA
BVOW11s1952071115

425651BV00002B/123/P